Spirit Filled Words

To Awaken the Sleeping Giant

JESSICA CAGER

BALBOA.
PRESS

A DIVISION OF HAY HOUSE

Balboa Press books may be ordered through booksellers or by contacting:

Balboa Press
A Division of Hay House
1663 Liberty Drive
Bloomington, IN 47403
www.balboapress.com
1 (877) 407-4847

Because of the dynamic nature of the Internet, any web addresses or links contained in this book may have changed since publication and may no longer be valid. The views expressed in this work are solely those of the author and do not necessarily reflect the views of the publisher, and the publisher hereby disclaims any responsibility for them.

The author of this book does not dispense medical advice or prescribe the use of any technique as a form of treatment for physical, emotional, or medical problems without the advice of a physician, either directly or indirectly. The intent of the author is only to offer information of a general nature to help you in your quest for emotional and spiritual well-being. In the event you use any of the information in this book for yourself, which is your constitutional right, the author and the publisher assume no responsibility for your actions.

Any people depicted in stock imagery provided by Thinkstock are models, and such images are being used for illustrative purposes only.
Certain stock imagery © Thinkstock.

Printed in the United States of America.

ISBN: 978-1-4525-9685-3 (sc)
ISBN: 978-1-4525-9687-7 (hc)
ISBN: 978-1-4525-9686-0 (e)

Library of Congress Control Number: 2014907834

Balboa Press rev. date: 5/30/2014

Introduction

These writings were inspired through pain and heartache. However, the outcome of each devotion ends in a dynamic win. First and foremost, I would like to thank our most precious Lord Jesus Christ. It is He who has inspired and compelled me to write a book such as this. While I was on my sickbed and could not speak, I found the almighty God's strength within to write. Through my journey with the Lord, I found true intimacy with Him. I have questioned many things that have occurred in my life. Nevertheless, the Spirit of the Lord has aided me in propelling myself through the raging waters of life. In these writings are personal struggles and battles of mine along with those of loved ones. May the sufferings and afflictions along with the trials and tribulations I have endured give you hope in your walk with God. Be blessed, and may these devotions penetrate your spirit, that you shall never be the same. Thanks be to God.

Epic 1

The Creator, heavenly Father, the Mighty One in battle,
there is none like You, forevermore and
always with Your children.
A God of might, power, excellence, and
honor. Who can measure up
to the Holy One of Israel?

Valor, honor, and praise is due to You, O Holy One,
for what man or gods can withstand
Your anointing, Your wrath,
and Your impeccable power?

No god or gods will ever compare to Father God.
Father, Your love is kind, winsome, and gracious.
Your love conquers all and surpasses all loneliness.

The deep and yearning affection I
have for You, O Great One, is
everlasting and serene.
My Lord, Your love is so powerful and
ecstatic that I feel Your warm
presence and peace; it stirs my soul and spirit.

How I long to be in Your presence.
How long must I wait until I see Your
beautiful angelic hands and face,
Father God?

Longing to be with You, my Husband,
My Father, my Counselor, my Redeemer.
Longing to have a deep and intimate
relationship with my Creator.

O Lord, Lord forever and eternally,
Lord of heaven and earth and
King of Glory,
Your children are yearning and waiting
patiently for Your glory.

Your strong glory, the Lord of justice, our vindicator.
Your heavenly children, Father God, are
eagerly waiting for the latter rain.

You reign over all.
You have power, might, and tremendous strength
to command the seas and the winds to cease.

As magnificent and powerful as You
are, Almighty One of Israel,
roaming over the seas and Your Spirit
hovering over the dark sky,
I yearn to be in the Almighty's presence.

A God of war, a God who sees and knows all,
a God who is Protector and Savior.
When You speak, Master, when You
breathe, Master, Your words break
all barriers and hindrances.

Take me to that place, my secret hiding place,
where we can have an intimate, loving
Father-and-daughter session.
You are my King; I am Your princess.
A most wonderful and endearing King
who would do anything for His
princess.

You are the best, You are the best Dad—
what more could I want?
You breathed Your powerful and mighty Spirit into my body.

Existing before the clouds, stars, moon,
sun, and other cosmic things,
Your Spirit was hovering over the world.
The great, powerful, and mighty Spirit of
God, roaming to and fro oceans,
seas, and gardens, creating magnificent places and things.

Glory, honor, praise, and blessing of
the Lord our God is upon my
life and future generations to come.

The Author, the Finisher, the Alpha and
Omega. My, what an awesome God
You are, knowing my life from beginning until the end!

A journey that has just begun with my Father.
I have many years left, but when my
awesome Father guides my steps into
my God-given destiny, I am in awe.

O Holy One of Israel, whatever call I have on my life,
Lord, You will hold my hand.
You will annihilate anyone who tries to harm Your children.
Lord who is pure in all Your ways, I will be with You on earth
and in heaven!

Epic 2

My heart and my soul cry to You, O Holy One of Israel.
Tears of sadness and melancholy stream
down my face into a large
puddle of grief,
wondering, will my soul and spirit be at peace?

The God of Abraham, glorious in all His ways,
though my flesh cries aloud and wants
to give into temptation,
the Lord who is mighty in battle will forever hold me up!

Daggers, knives, and swords are aiming at my soul and spirit.
These weapons of evil are trying to
defeat a mighty woman of
the heavenly Creator.
Satan's weapons are no match for the
armor and artillery that Jehovah
Jireh has placed in me.

The wolves and the blood-sucking devils
roam in the midnight hour,
preying on my soul and immortal body.
These detestable creatures are trying
to destroy God's children.
The Lord Almighty and the angels of
His armies encamp around
me with fire and mighty swords.

Though I may be running for dear life,
the King above all kings is sending His
horses along with chariots
of fire to vindicate my soul.

Walking through darkness and dark, murky swamps,
the God Almighty surrounds me with His dynamic arms.
The God of power illuminates this
dreadful world with His awesome
light.

Flesh wants to give in, the words of
my mouth want to give in,
but my inner being will never give in.
My spirit and soul will always and
forevermore be linked to my
heavenly Father.

In times of turmoil and distress, I know the Creator will be
my vindicator.

Tough times do not last, but tough people do.
Rocks, stones, and thorns may attack my physical body,
but no harm will come to my immortal
spirit because God is my Protector.

Epic 3

My spirit and soul will always praise You forevermore.
Oh, how I enjoy and marvel at glorifying Your precious name!
Beautiful You are, O Lord, and
magnificent in all righteousness.
How I yearn to see the creature's face.
How I yearn to live in Your divine and awesome presence.
I can never stop giving the almighty God praise and glory.

Heavenly Father, I love how we just dance for hours and days.
My heart eagerly waits for Your return.
My heart so eager to know my Father's heart.

My inner man is always ecstatic and joyful when in the
Almighty's presence.
I surrender all to You, my body, soul, and spirit.

The atmosphere of heaven is impeccable.
Rubies, emeralds, diamonds, sapphires,
and other precious stones,
created by my Father, surround His throne.

Fire and horses with chariots of fire
surround the Mighty One in
battle.
When the Creator speaks, the universe,
earth, even sea monsters
all quiver at the sound of the Lord's voice.

Michael, Gabriel, David, and Jesus
encamp around the Holy One
of Israel.
Men of valor, honor, and courage,
praising and worshipping our
omnipotent God.

My Father's words and His ways are
the treasures of my heart.
His understanding and ways are all but a mystery to man.
Man may never know God's ways,
but a righteous and God-fearing man will know the secrets of
God's heart.

The heart of the Father, pure and holy
yet a deep and profound
mystery.
Man and science try rigorously to know the Father's heart,
but only those hungry for wisdom will
know the heavenly Father's
heart.

When one find's the heart of Christ, he will be
foreverrmore attached to His bosom.
My heart and my Father's heart are
joined together for all eternity.

God's heart is like a diamond surrounded
by the crown of favor.
The Father's heart, so pure and so rich in holiness.
The King's heart, powerful yet gentle.

Your hand, compassionate yet fierce and mighty.
In my Father's hands are strength and
wisdom like never before.
In my Father's hands is power to do the impossible.

The Mighty One's hand is on my life, my children, and future
generations to come.
Might, power, valor, and tenacity flow
from the heavenly Father
to my spirit.

The hands of God are against those who wrong His children.
The King's hands roam to and fro the
earth, bringing healing and
restoration to His people.
Beast nor man can withstand the power in His hands.

Miracles, signs, and wonders man cannot explain,
nor the God above every god and the King who rules over all.
A just God, nothing can defeat His divine presence.

A divine presence that will be left on
earth and across the seas.
A divine presence that will be with me, even in my grave.

Epic 4

Jesus, oh, how You are such a wonderful
and dear Husband to me!
The almighty God, who is my Husband, a Man of tenacity,
honor, glory, strength, and wisdom.
Dear Husband, I thank You for feeding
my soul with spiritual food.

A Husband who is at one with His precious wife.
My dearest Husband, how we are
connected in mind, body, and
spirit.
Our spirits are conjoined for all eternity,

Combined in flesh, combined in spirit, combined in soul.
Father God, I thank You for filling Your princess with
unconditional love.

We are linked together on earth and in heaven.
Though I cannot touch Your angelic
face, Your divine presence
stirs my soul.

My Husband comforts me as tears stream from my eyes,
a Husband that instills godly wisdom and revelation to
my spirit.
A Husband that keeps His dynamic
hands on my soul and spirit.

As I sit by my Husband on His throne surrounded by angels
with fire,
I worship my One and only true Husband,
Listening and in awe as my Husband speaks words that man
cannot comprehend.

I give praise and honor to my Husband walking through the
streets of Jerusalem to the tabernacle.
I worship my Husband in the beauty of His holiness.

A Husband who breathes His wisdom and knowledge into my
spirit so we are one in unity.
A Husband who instructs and leads His wife to holiness and
reverence.

As I listen to my Husband's sermons, my
spirit and soul are lightened.
My Husband's wisdom and righteousness enlightens and stirs
my inner being.

Oh, how I marvel at dancing with my
Husband on heaven's diamond
and gold roads,
dancing into all eternity as my spirit and soul yearn for my
Husband's understanding.

A Husband who is impeccable, free from sin and full of
righteousness. Pure in all His ways,
the love of my Husband supersedes all carnal love.
A love that puts peace and joy in my spirit.

Carnal love dies, but my Husband's love lasts for eternity.

Epic 5

Walking through the streets of Jerusalem,
hearing the elders spread
the good news,
I go to my Father's house, which is in His tabernacle.
Approaching the doors, I can feel the Spirit of God
descending upon me as I open them.

My soul and spirit are in awe of the magnificent creations of
my Father.
The floors are marble and gold beset with diamonds.
The windows are glass with images of
David, Gabriel, and Michael.

Walking farther toward the altar, I see angels with white
robes and swords surrounding the almighty God.
How powerful these angels are, as the God Almighty
breathes His wisdom and the angels come minister to me.

How I dazzle waking up every morning, going to the
tabernacle.
Inside are three thrones—one for the
Father, one for the Son, and one for the Holy Spirit.
I bow down in reverence to the Father, and
stand in awe as the Father, Son, and Holy
Spirit prophesy to me.

I lift my hands in praise and worship
and kneel, fearing the Father.
As I lay on His precious floor, His divine
presence lifts my mortal body.

Man may never know and experience the Father's
presence,
But the children of God Almighty knows and
understands the power that is within the Father.

As I walk through the tabernacle, holding hands
with the Father,
He opens this door, and my eyes become blinded
because of the glory that surrounds my Father.

As I open my eyes, the Father has removed my spirit
from earth and translated it into heaven so I
may see His mysteries.

The mortal man may think he knows God's will
and mysteries
But only the true and God-fearing warriors of God
know the mysteries that indwell the Father's heart.

As my spirit is walking with the Father, I see
many books filled with the names of people who have and
who will do remarkable things in the name of Jesus.

A treasure chest is surrounded by David and Gabriel.
As it opens, eyes and ears have not seen or heard
the glory and strong downpour of hidden mysteries
that God will reveal to His chosen people.

As the Spirit of God lifts me up, the Father takes
me on a journey deeper into the treasure chest where
knowledge, revelation, insight, wisdom, and
discernment like never before are hidden.

My eyes and ears stare in amazement at the hidden
treasures.
God's heart is a treasure.
When one seeks the heart of the Father, many
mysteries will be revealed to the spirit of His
child.

Oh, how I yearn to live in my Father's tabernacle.
The wisdom and knowledge of the Father are
embedded in my spirit and soul.
Though flesh and blood cannot see the Father,
my spiritual eyes will have divine encounters with
my Father like never before.

Epic 6

God's wrath is kindled against those who have done
His children wrong.
God's wrath, dynamic yet so effective.
My Father's wrath is no match for beast or man.

The Father is against Satan and his army.
The Father is impeccable yet is a destroyer of nations
that come against His people.
God's anger and wrath are kindled against dark
beings and images.

My Father will soon return for His children.
The Father in heaven is training His warriors
for combat.
The Father's warriors are clothed with brass and
fine metal.

The armor exudes confidence.
The armor is embroidered by the hand of the
Father, symbolizing strength and power.

Walking out of heaven's palace and through the
crystalline gates,
the God Almighty assigns every angel a specific
horse for a God-given task.
The horses of God's army are clothed in heavy brass
with wings of fire.

As I look above, the heavens are now open.
I see mighty warriors with dynamic swords on
horses of fire.
A loud and boisterous noise from heaven shakes
the earth,
a noise that signals fear in God's enemies' hearts.
Thunder, lightning, and the horses sound the return
for the Mighty One in battle.

The Father in His chariot is surrounded
by horses that stand thirty feet tall.
The Father's eyes pierce through my soul.
His hands firmly grip the ropes of righteousness
and power.

Who or what being can understand the mind of the Father?
The enslaved man to Satan has no access to the Father's
wisdom.
A man pricked in his heart by the Holy Spirit has all the
wisdom and mysteries revealed to him.

Man and science rationalize through their natural and
unclean minds when the Father will return.
The Father will return like a mighty wind in the midnight
hour.

Armageddon but a few miles away,
Death and ghouls will cover the souls and spirits
of God's enemies.
Wolves and serpents will howl the midnight hour for
uncleanness.

The righteous are taken into the Father's bosom.
The righteous on the angels' horses.
God's children will be at rest with their Father in
heaven.
The Father's mighty hand is hovering over the righteous
as His Spirit annihilates earth and hades.

Epic 7

The Father's anger is malicious and infectious to
those who do evil.
God's anger is against those who rape and steal the
Word from His children.
God's anger is against evil in holy places.

Man and beast try to escape the Mighty One's
punishment.
God's fiery eyes roam to and fro the universe
and seas.
God is hovering over the universe.

God's Spirit is in dark and muddy places, tossing
ungodliness into the depths of hades.
Man may try to eliminate the Creator with man-made
science,

But the Holy One of Israel's Spirit will remain on earth even
after the battle of Armageddon.
Oh, how I groan and sigh for the spirits and souls of
unbelievers.

Father God, have mercy on them.
Have mercy and spare the lives of those who are ignorant
of the Word.
Spare their souls and spirits.

Prick them in their hearts, O Holy One.
Sprinkle Your unconditional love and righteousness
into their spirit man.

Father God, send Your angelic Spirit onto the streets and
into the houses of the unbelievers.
Show and manifest Your goodness, Lord, in the heart of
the unbeliever.

A man is not right in his heart once he is born.
Surrendering all to Christ, a man will be
pure in his spirit and walk with God.

Man is foolish in his ways.
Man believing his life is his own
is ignorant to the counsel and reverential fear of the Lord.

Man must get right with the Father before he can see the
fruits of his hands be blessed.
Blessed hands from the unjust judge are slothful and
empty in the sight of the Lord.

A righteous man's hands will prosper if God is the head
of his body.
Pure hands in the sight of the Lord is my heart's desire.

Heavenly Father, spread the blood of the Lamb on man's
mind, spirit, and soul.
The blood of the Lamb, pure from all impurities;
the blood of the Lamb, grafted on my mortal soul and
body.

Father, I yearn to know the power in the blood of the
Lamb.
God's chosen people are saturated in spirit and soul by
the blood of Jesus.

O heavenly Father, cleanse this house, my family, and
future generations to come with the blood of the Lamb.

Beautiful You are, Lord.
When one finds the beauty in the Father, it becomes
his treasure.

God's treasure is naked in the heart of the unbeliever.
But a righteous man in his heart has
God's treasure embedded
in his spirit and soul for eternity.

A man's treasure is in his heart, be it good or bad.
A righteous man's treasure is in the heart of God for
eternity.

Epic 8

As I look to the heavens with my natural eyes, I see a
powder-blue sky.
Hurting internally, my flesh saying, "God does not hear
you,"
my spirit is at work with the Father, building my inner
man.

Life is but a dream, and life is yet a mystery to the man who
does not know the Father.
The trials and tribulations of life are trying to eat away at
me.
Yet the Father, not physically visible, is visible in my spirit.

Satan and his army are throwing fiery darts at my mind and
flesh.
But God's sword is dynamic with fire, surrounding the sword.
Satan and his ghouls are inferior to the Master's weaponry.

Riding alongside the Father, encamped by chariots of
fire,
the Father raises the sword and the devils run in terror and
in torment.

Satan is trying to bring down a mighty warrior of God.
Satan is no match for the terror I will cause in his
kingdom.

God's mysteries are profound yet impactful on the
spirit of the believer.
Mysteries, knowledge, and wisdom are divine endowments
of the Father.
Father, release Your revelation into the spirits of Your
children.

The keys to the Father's mysteries are hidden for the
righteous,
keys unlocking warfare and artillery like never before—
an infantry of God's warriors, machines created by the
Father, weaponry surpassing the unjust judge's mind, and
tanks made of iron—surrounded by the shield of favor.

Horses are wearing the helmet of salvation.
Michael and Gabriel, ten feet tall with the hands
of the Father encamping them,

fire pours out of their mouths
as they defeat the devils.

Michael and Gabriel are masters at warfare.
Michael and Gabriel at the Father's side are being
instilled with might that surpasses many centuries
to come.

The Father, Michael, and Gabriel are encamped around
my spirit; it is undefeatable, untouchable, and invisible.

Satan was defeated before he was created.
Hades will soon become annihilated,
and Satan's devils shall be executed by the angels of
God's army.

The Father is forever in existence.
The Father, whose power no foe can withstand.
The Almighty is on the throne for eternity.
The Master, annihilating hades before it was
created.

The Father's kingdom is superb in all its ways.
Satan is a weakling in the Father's eyes.
The Master, the Creator, and the Almighty, glorious
yet powerful before the universe existed.

Epic 9

Heavenly Father, I come to Your throne kneeling and
bowing, giving reverence and worship to Your holy
name.

Father, I thirst to see Your angelic face.
Father, my spirit thirsts to be in Your presence for
eternity.

How I want to sit at Your feet.
The Almighty's feet are pure and holy.
Feet of gold are surrounded by a heavy downpour
of glory.

My soul is longing to touch and kiss Your hands,
hands of gold and bronze.
The Father's hands have two bronze rings bordered
with diamonds.
The rings symbolize the ferocious power in the Almighty's
hands.

As I touch the Father's hands, His anointing struck my
spirit.
Power and might are injected into my inner being.

My spirit soared to a divine level,
A divine level where the deep and secret things are not
understood by the natural mind.

A foolish man will never experience a superabundant level of divine power.
Man, believing his thoughts and ways are superior to the Majesty's,
is a foolish man in his heart, believing
that he is his own man.

A God-fearing man abides in the shadow of the Almighty.
A man of God respects and honors his Father's words.
A righteous man allows the Father to abide in his spirit so the Father will mold him into a walking god.

Man is lost in spirit and mind.
Man is ravaging the country for provision.
Mankind is lost in the darkness.

A foolish man is cut off from the spirit realm.
A righteous man's light is bright, warning away all devils.
A righteous man is conjoined with the Father in spirit.
A righteous man bows to the Father for godly wisdom.

In the last days, an unsaved man will become a primitive beast.
An ungodly man will allow Satan to dictate his mind and spirit.
A foolish man in the eyes of the Almighty is in his grave.

A godly man, endlessly fearing the Lord,
A righteous man takes refuge in His Father's palace.
A Christlike man crucifies the flesh, yet he dwells in the spirit realm eternally.

Man is desperately seeking a way out.
Man's spirit is angered at his slothful life.
Mankind is weak in spirit and provision.

Man's inner being has to get right with the Father.
Man must open his heart to the Father if he wants to see
the fruits of his labor blessed.
The spirit of darkness must die if man wants eternal
salvation.

Man roams the streets howling for God's children,
a man perverse in heart, mind, and spirit.
An ungodly man rapes the weak of their strength.

Christ's Spirit hovers over the brokenhearted.
Christ redeems people's lives with unconditional love.
Christ holds our hands as we walk through a dark
and horrific world.

My spirit is destined and determined to see the power
of His resurrection.
I am hungering to see His glory on earth.
My spirit and soul cries for everlasting salvation.

A divine presence is my heart's desire,
my inner hope for deity in the final days.
The days on earth are terminated, but days
in heaven are endless.
Though I have an earthly mom and dad, my spirit
is with my heavenly Father forever.

Epic 10

Walking through the streets of Jerusalem,
my spirit is destined to see the walls of Jericho.

Standing in awe with my Father, I see a vision of
Joshua and Kaleb.
Joshua, tall in stature with brown hair and piercing blue
eyes;
Joshua's skin golden as the sun sets in the west.

Joshua is dressed in brass armor with a symbol of
the Father's hand on his breastplate.
Sitting behind him is a warrior angel ministering to
Joshua on which way to go.

Alongside the horse is the Holy Spirit.
The Holy Spirit is guiding the angels' every move.

The enemy is charging Joshua head-on.
Joshua is confident in God Almighty.
The enemy tries to slay Joshua, but the Father's
Spirit overtakes the enemy.

The Mighty One in battle covers their enemies with
shame.
The Master is dynamic and undefeatable.

The Father and Joshua are united in mind, body, and spirit.
The Father and Joshua are inseparable.
God the Father is the head of Joshua's life.

The Father has instilled might and power into Joshua that no devil can confiscate.
The feet of Joshua are blessed by the Father's Spirit.
Joshua's feet are a monument in history.
The footsteps of a God-fearing man are rooted on earth and in heaven.

Epic 11

Father, I pray that Your Spirit delights in my presence,
my spirit.
My soul is thirsting for the knowledge of God.
Father, my heart is weary from the trials and
tribulations.

My flesh, my body, and my appearance are weakened
from the unjust judge's afflictions.
My eyes grow heavy and gloomy.
The mortal body is growing faint from the thorns
and thistles.

My weakened body is striving for strength.
The inner man is ferocious as a lion's roar.
My arms ache from battling the unjust judge.

Crushed under the unjust judge's feet,
my spirit and soul strengthen me to pray at the
altar.
Tears of sadness from a weakening and melancholy
heart stream down Thy face.

The Mighty One grabs His daughter's hand.
Divine energy, power, and strength travels to my
immortal spirit.
Power! Power from the almighty God!

The unjust judge has afflicted my life with
snakes and serpents.
The unjust judge is throwing fiery darts at my head,
my body, and my life.
The accuser is wreaking havoc on God's children.

Tests and trials are coming my way.
Obstacles and wars like never before.
The battle between a mighty woman of God
and Satan.

The Lord is my vindicator.
The Master fights my battles.
The battle is not mine; it is the Lord's.

Beaten and stoned I may be,
persecuted and defamed for serving Jesus
Christ.
Family, friends, and people of the congregation
conspire for my downfall.

Many will turn their backs to me,
but no one can ever take the love of my
Father from my heart, nor the power of
God that abides within me.

Epic 12

My flesh and heart are running from my
Father.
My spirit and soul want to go into the
Father's bosom.
Flesh and spirit are at war with one another.

Endless days and endless nights are filled
with sorrow.
My eyes and flesh are lusting after ungodly
creatures.
The spirit man cries aloud for purification and
sanctification in Christ.

The God Almighty has put a powerful call upon
my life and my descendants.
The Master's Spirit hovers over my immortal spirit.
The Father has called me before I entered my
mother's womb.

The ungodly creatures lust after a man of God.
The wolves and the crows roam the streets for
my spirit.
The spirits of infirmity, sickness, and disease
seek my life.

I hide my face and my unclean flesh from the
Father.
Despair and melancholy cover my soul and
spirit.
My life and my eyes are enslaved by darkness.

I, Your son, Father God, have disowned and
disobeyed Your commandments.
Your commandments, Father, are buried with me
in the place of Sheol.
A servant of the Mighty One is captured in the
kingdom of darkness.

Curses, enchantments, and divinations are piercing
my mortal body.
The unjust judge's army is rising to conspire
against my life.

The unjust judge is putting borders and fences
around my mind.

I am lost in the wilderness.
The spirit of lying runs my soul.
The spirit of lust fills my eyes
The spiritual eyes are blinded by deceit and
mistrust.

God and Satan are determined for my life.
The Devil wants my gifts for the advancement
of his kingdom,
but the Almighty has a plan for my life that is
predestined.

Heavenly Father, rescue me from the place of
Sheol.
Father God, extend Your mighty arm of valor
upon my life.
O Holy One of Israel, infect my spirit with
righteousness and tenacity.

Father, shine Your Spirit upon my soul.
The Creator of heaven and earth, cleanse me
of all unrighteousness.
Master, instill me with a heart that loves only
You.

My spirit man is dead.
I, Your son, am sleeping.
My spirit and soul are slaves in the kingdom
of darkness.

The Enemy and his army are unbeatable in
human strength.
When my Father resurrects my spirit from the
dead, I will be undefeatable.
My Father has put a powerful anointing on my
life.

The power of the Father has raised my spirit.
God's mighty hand surrounds me like a shield.
The Father has saturated my inner man with the
oil of joy.

You are my King, I am Your prince. I will avenge
God's children who have been oppressed.
You arm Your prince with honor, valor, courage,
and might.

The Father has stirred a power in me that no
devil can withstand.
Your son will conquer many things and people.
The Father has anointed me to ravage Satan's
kingdom.

The divine presence of God is upon my life.
The power of God will flow through my hands
and bring many nations to Christ.
The mighty words from the Father will flow
through my mouth and annihilate Satan.

Epic 13

The day of the Lord is near the earth.
The return of the Father is but days away.
Man must decide to serve the Farther or
remain in darkness.

The Lord is raising young men and women from
all nations.
The chosen ones are bowing and giving reverence
to the Father night and day.
The anointed people of God will rule the earth.

The fall of Satan and his angles is coming soon.
Satan's kingdom will be ravaged by walking
gods.
These walking gods will defeat nations like
never before in name of Jesus.

Jesus will return like a thief in the night.
Within the blink of an eye, man's soul and
spirit will be judged by the Almighty.
Man must surrender all to the Father if he
wants eternal life.

The gift of eternal life and salvation are
fruits of the Spirit from the Father.
My everlasting spirit is longing to be in
paradise with my Father.
The spirits of God's children are in paradise.

Mankind rationalizes in his natural ability of
what paradises looks like.
The heart of an evil man will never know the
mysteries to everlasting paradise.
A man pricked in his heart by the Holy Spirit
will have encounters with paradise like never
before.

The natural eyes are blinded by Satan and
his fallen angels.
The spiritual eyes see what the wicked cannot.
The wicked hovers over the spirit of the lost.

Wicked beings roam the cities for uncleanness.
The wicked are like the dogs of the night,
growling and gnarling the weak.
The wicked grow mighty in Satan's kingdom.

The chosen one from the Father's heart goes from
glory and reaches new levels of favor.
The kingdom of God is eternal.
The kingdom of God will reign for centuries
to come.
The kingdom of God will put the kingdom of
darkness beneath its feet.

A righteous man commands the spirit of
strength and courage.
A man of God will bring shame upon Satan and
his family; by following the Holy Spirit,
a righteous man in his mother's womb is
filled with the Holy Spirit.

God the Father crowns his sons and daughters
with glory and favor.
The favor of God covers the righteous like a
shield.

God's chosen ones are engrafted in the Father's
heart.
The Father's heart is a mystery to the unsaved
man,
but a saved man is conjoined with the Father's heart.

The natural man's heart is torn between God and
Satan.
A wicked man's heart is bound to the torment of
hades.
A wicked man indulges in lust, tormenting
the righteous, and capturing the eyes of the weak.

A God-fearing man seeks the Father's guidance.
A man of God will torment Satan and his kingdom.
A man of God has a bright light that shines forth
in demonic places.

I am one with my Father.
Wherever my soul goes, the Father's Spirit encamps
my flesh and my inner being.
I am joined with my Father in spirit, in heaven and on earth.

Epic 14

The vengeance of the Lord is upon those who
have shamed His children.
This will be the year of vengeance like never before.
My God will avenge His children.

The Father's anger is kindled against the wicked.
The wicked have tormented and put God's people
to shame for years.
God's anger will be mightier than ever.

The Mighty One will clothe the demons and
unfamiliar spirits with a power that is undefeatable.
The spirits of torment and oppression will be cast
into the pit of hades by the Father.
The Father will come forth like a wind, ravaging
many nations.

Many nations and the wicked will fall by the sword
of the Almighty.
The hand of the Almighty is more ferocious than the
roar of a lion.
The Father will raise both hands and command storms
to annihilate the wickedness in nations.

The Father is preparing for war.
The Almighty has artillery and infantry that nations
have yet to see.
My Master is raising an army of warriors of God
like never before.

God's warriors have spirits of giants.
These giants are no match for the kingdom of
darkness.
These giants of the Mighty One are falling
from heaven.

The giants of God are assigned to the chosen ones.
The ones called by God have giants of God on their
side like never before.
God is infecting his leaders with the giant spirit.

God's giants will avenge the deaths of the Father's
children.
These warriors of God are encamped by wings
of fire.

The wings of fire can withstand all the forces
of darkness.
The wings of fire are breathed out of the Father's
mouth.
The wings of fire will terminate all abominations
in the name of Jesus.

The Father's eyes covers His children from harm.
The Father's eyes will penetrate the heart and soul
of the wicked.
The eyes of the Father are ravaging the spirit of
the wicked.

The Father is raising disastrous waters.
These waters are after the souls of the wicked.
God will cause the sea and the sea monsters to
feed upon the flesh of the wicked.

The day of vengeance is inescapable for the
wicked.
God's wrath and vengeance are no match for
man, beast, or spirit.
The sovereign ruler will breathe fiery coals on
the wicked.

The Lord is my vindicator.
Vengeance belongs to the Lord.
The Lord will return with might and power
like never before.
The adversary will be clothed will shame
and destitution.

All havoc and torment will be upon Satan and
his army.
The Father in these last days will torment the
mind of Satan.
The unjust judge shall be no more!

Epic 15

Father God, the son in my womb will leave a
presence on earth.
Heavenly Father, I thank You for crowning my
son as a prince.
Father, I thank You for crowning my son, Your
Son, as a king on earth.

The Almighty One will pour His Spirit upon my
son, who is in my womb.
You have anointed my son with the oil of joy.
Your prince will always praise and give glory
to His King.

The Master has created my son before earth was
formed.
A son and His Father are joined in holy matrimony,
a unification of the Spirit of the Father and a son
never to be broken

O Holy One of Israel, I thank You for calling my
son a warrior in Your army.
Though my son has an earthly father, the Creator is
his true Father.
You have crowned my son with riches that supersede
the natural eye.

Father God, You have clothed Your son in fine
linen along with shoes of power and might.
The fine linen represents Your son's purity and
consecration in Christ.

Christ is the head of my son.
My son is married to Christ in spirit.

The church was embedded in my son's heart
before the heaven's existed.
My son will forevermore be married to the
church.

The love of Christ in my son's heart is everlasting.
His Father is instilling godly wisdom and
revelation that supersedes man's heart.
The wisdom of man in the Almighty's eyes
is perverse and wicked.

The son that God has borne to me will ravage
many countries and nations.
The strength of the almighty God flows
through my son like a peaceful river.
The strength of my son will demolish and
deplete the souls and spirits of the wicked.

The hand of the Lord is upon my son and
his descendants.
The angels of the Lord surround a mighty
warrior of God.
The hand of the Lord and His angels will lift
my son in times of persecution.

Words of hate and deceit will attack my son.
Sickness and disease from the pit of hell will
try to pour their way into my son's spirit.
Nations will rise against my son to bring
him to nonexistence.

The Lord will avenge my son of his persecutions
and afflictions.
The Almighty will turn my son's tears into tears
of happiness.
The Holy One will move His Spirit upon my
son's behalf.

Attacks of bodily harm and death may seek
my son's life.
Spells, curses, and witchcraft are aimed at God's
precious son.
The unjust judge will hunt for the soul and spirit
of God's anointed son.

Though I am carrying the seed of Abraham in
my womb, the Father will fight on the behalf
of my son.
The Father will raise my son to spoil Satan and
his army.
My son will start a movement like never before.

A movement of justice and vengeance God will
shine forth in my son's spirit like never before.
My son will torment and taunt the wicked even
as they sleep.
My son will command devils to flee from His
presence in the name of Jesus.

God has called forth my son to spread the good news.
My son will leave a legacy for many centuries to come.
The Father will set my son up on many nations.
People and devils will bow at the knee of my son because the Living God is in his spirit and the divine presence of the Lord is upon his life.

Epic 16

Though thorns and thistles may attack my mortal
being, the inner man glorifies in affliction because
the Almighty has increased my strength.
Blessed be the name of God forever and ever
because the Father will always come to the rescue
of His children.

The trials and the tribulations of Satan weaken the
human spirit and flesh.
But when the power of His resurrection enters our spirits,
it glorifies the Father.
Yearning, thriving souls and spirits for the Lord
increase in divine connection with the Father like
never before.

Afflictions and persecutions of the just are inevitable,
but the power of God within us is everlasting.
The power of the Father terminates all evil and wickedness.

The heart of an unsaved woman is treacherous and
vindictive.
An unsaved woman, used by Satan, is an abomination
to the Father.
An unsaved woman allows the devils to feed on her
unclean body.

A capable, virtuous, and intelligent woman strives
for the knowledge of her Husband.
A godly woman cherishes her body because it
is the temple of Christ.
A woman pure in heart will see the manifestation
of Christ.

Wickedness covers the soul and spirit of an evil woman.
An evil woman allows Satan to guide her spirit to
manipulate the just.
The just are blinded by the sweet and pleasant smile
of Jezebel.

A woman of Jezebel is thrown into the pit of hell by the
Father.
The Father torments Jezebel's spirit because of
her wickedness.
A woman of Jezebel is taunted in mind by the
Spirit.

The Father delights in holiness and sanctification.
The Almighty desires purification in the body
of Christ.
The body of Christ is dead spiritually when it comes
to purification and sanctification.

The Holy One of Israel pleasures His Spirit in a
body of purity.
Purity is what the Holy Spirit desires in God's
children.
The holy water in God's heart is what I desire.

The water in the Father's heart quenches my
spiritual being.
My soul is determined to be filled with holy water.
This powerful water increases my strength in the
Father.

My Father has cleansed me from all unrighteousness.
The Father has filled my immortal spirit with
pure water.
This pure water has cleansed all of my iniquities
and infirmities.

Heavenly Father, send a downpour of Your holy
water.
O Holy One of Israel, Your children are thirsting
for Your truth.
Your truth is my deliverance from all bondage
and oppression.

Father, thank You for pouring water on thirsting
ground.
The ground of my inner man longs for everlasting
holy water.
The Father's holy water is a precious gemstone
in my soul.

My soul cries, "Abba Father!"
My heart is pricked by the Holy Spirit's anointing.
God's pure water and anointing flow like
a calm river in my spirit.

My inner man is destined to be in heaven
with my Father.
The Father's power and might dwells in the
presence of righteousness.
The flesh is ignorant to righteousness, but my
spirit is in right standing with the Lord.

The Lord's path is perfect.
Satan's path is destructive and disastrous.
When one finds the Father's love, one will
have everlasting peace and rest.

Epic 17

My spirit and soul are enslaved to Satan
and his mighty army.
The wolves of the night are after my soul.
The unjust judge lurks the cities of the ungodly
for my mind, body, and spirit.

My flesh and spirit are at war with the Father.
The Father's hands are open for my return.
My Father desires intimacy from within.

O Holy One, I cry in distress.
My heart and mind are under attack.
Satan has a stronghold on a mighty man
of God.
The unjust judge has my spirit chained from
the truth.

The spirit of Jezebel torments my mind.
Jezebel has cursed my entire being.
The curse from Jezebel is mightier than
my spirit.

The descendants of Jezebel lash my spirit
and soul with wickedness.
This ungodly woman has clawed my face and
left scars of torment and torture.

Jezebel and her false prophets are planning
my demise.
The spirit of Jezebel hovers over my mortal body
like a ravenous wolf.
This unclean woman has united her wicked soul with
my soul.

Through sleepless and endless nights,
I am tormented and haunted by her presence.
This descendant of Jezebel utters slander and
blasphemy about the Master.

Days, months, and years of pain, along with agony
from Satan.
The Devil has sent this evil woman to destroy a
mighty man of God.
The Devil and his fallen angels conspire for the
anointing on my life.
Eyes and ears have not seen or heard about the
vengeance of the Lord.
The Creator is my vindicator.
The Father will save my soul from the lion's mouth.

The mouth of the lion has devoured my inner being.
The lion is lying and waiting for my soul in hades.
The fallen angels are rejoicing in hades over my
weakened spirit and soul.

The spirits of humiliation, shame, and agony cover
my appearance.
My eyes are saddened and weakened.
My inner man is crushed by the unjust judge.

The spirit of fear and treachery haunt my life.
Satan has evoked his army to abuse my spirit
and my soul.
My soul is but a day away from the grave.

The spirit of death wants my soul.
Death howls through the hallways of my house.
This inhumane spirit hovers over a mighty warrior.

O Father, save me from the lion's mouth.
My Lord, avenge my spirit from the adversary.

God, I am lost in the darkness.
My flesh is terrified of surrendering to
the Almighty.
The Almighty wants me to surrender all.
I am afraid of the call on my life.

The Father has given me a powerful call.
Though I run in terror and dismay, my spirit
is with the Father in heaven.
Pull my spirit from hades, Father, and put me
in Your bosom.

My spirit is longing to be home with the Father.
I am weary and faint from running from my God-
given destiny.
My arms grow weak from battling the unjust judge.

O Holy One of Israel, be my comforter.
I desire to be in the secret place of the Most
High God.
Send the spirits of gentleness, love, and unconditional
companionship.

Father God, remove the tears of melancholy.
Wash away the tears of grief.
Cleanse my body with the blood of the Lamb and
holy water.

Heavenly Father, I am willing to crucify the old spirit.
The old spirit is dead. Breathe Your Spirit upon my
flesh.
Send forth Your divine presence and Your light.

My soul desires to be free from this ungodly woman
and Satan.
Send Your sword to cut the chains of slavery.
I am willing to die internally for everlasting life.

My Father is calling me to be at peace.
Jesus, You are the Prince of Peace.
Father God, You said You would trade Your peace
for my peace.

I am redeemed from the blood of the Lamb.
My life is redeemed from the curses of this
enslaved world.
My worldly life has passed away.
I am a king in my Father's eyes.
I am a new creature in Christ. Old things
have passed away; behold all things become new.
The Father has stirred a hurricane of power in me
that eyes and ears have not seen or heard.

Epic 18

My spirit and soul have wandered away from
my Father.
I am lost in the darkness.
My soul and spirit have been enslaved by the
adversary.

Satan and his fallen angels have tied my soul from
truth.
The spirits of sickness, disease, and death have hunted
me like a slave.
Curses and vexations have cursed my mortal being.

The Father is welcoming his daughter with open arms.
My flesh desires the lustful things of this demonic world.
The inner man cries for purification and sanctification
in Christ.

My soul and spirit are torn.
The unjust judge has howled for my spirit.
In my mother's womb, Satan and his army have conspired
to annihilate me.

Days, nights, months, and years of distress and turmoil,
nights of pain and torture,
the spirit of suicide has longed for my life.

Ungodly creatures have haunted me in my dreams.
The spirits of sex and lust have a stronghold on my spirit.
The spirit of sex lurks the streets of the city for my soul.

My inner being has been ravaged by the adversary.
The fallen angels crowd around me with the snare of
the fowler.
Satan roams the city, seeking whom he may devour.

I have allowed Satan and his army to solicit my soul
for wealth.
Ungodly men have preyed on my mortal being for pleasure.
The devils have found pleasure in feeding on my spirit.

Father God, my spirit and soul are aching.
Your daughter has been abused and violated by Satan.
Satan has put thorns and thistles in my spiritual being.

I cry, "Abba Father, save me from the place of the dead."
O Holy One of Israel, pick me up with Your mighty
hand.
My Lord, my spirit and soul are weak.

O Father God, Your daughter wants to restore
fellowship.
Heal and mend my broken heart.
My heart cries in pain and agony.
My heart is but a few moments from death.

Cleanse me from all unrighteousness.
Heavenly Father, wash me in the blood of Jesus.
Fill me with unconditional love the way a father loves
his daughter.

I am the walking dead.
My soul and spirit are perishing from the lashes of
Satan.
The inner man is dying because of the wickedness
done to me.

Fill me with Your power, God.
I am willing to be crucified to be with my Father.
Father, annihilate my soul and spirit along with the
ungodly soul ties.

Crucify my flesh so I may be one with my Father.
My Father has turned my mourning into joy.
Satan no longer has control over this woman of God.

I have been raped and beaten spiritually by Satan.
Satan has left me for dead.

I am returning to my Father.
The Lord is my vindicator.
My God shall never put His people to shame.
The power that raised Christ from the dead
has raised me the dead.

I am determined to know the power of His resurrection.
I am filled with the Godhead;
I am filled with the Holy Spirit.

My Father is raising me in the midst of chaos.
I and my Father are one.
The Father has sent me to strip Satan of his wealth.

I will annihilate the kingdom of darkness.
My Father's power within me will torment Satan
even in his grave.

Epic 19

Heavenly Father, I come into Your courts with
praise and thanksgiving.
My mouth shall continually praise You.
I thank You, Father, for protecting my house from
demonic attack.

My house was built on satanic ground.
The ghouls howled around my house like ravenous
wolves.
This house was once possessed because of the wickedness
in the ground.

The ground beneath the house poisoned the foundation
of the house as well inside.
Many sacrifices and séances have been held on the ground
of my house.
Ungodly creatures of the night evoked spiritual beings
from the pit of hell.

Disastrous winds and tornadoes have formed within this
house as well as without.
A monstrous disease has lurked this ground for centuries.
The people who once evoked wickedness are now
perishing in hades.

My house has been the center of attacks.
The foundation of this house and the ground have cried
for freedom.
This house was once tormented and taunted by evil beings.

Wicked people have cursed this house.
People dressed as good shepherds of the Lord were hiding
demons in their souls.
Many people have left ungodly beings in my house.

These demoniacs have waited for centuries to attack a
house of the Lord.
The Lord is against those who have done His children
wrong.
The Lord's anger is kindled against all wickedness.

The wickedness has hunted my spirit before I was
formed in my mother's womb.
My house was once a prison to a disciple of
Jesus Christ.
Though wickedness has covered my house, the monsters
of Satan cannot remove the Father, who is in my heart.

Evil men of the night have lurked around my house.
The demons have sat on my porch and waited for my
mother's and my spirits.
Wicked men have latched onto the foundation of this
house.

The fallen angels once crawled through the doors and
windows of this dwelling.
My house was covered in shame because of the wicked
done on this soil.
This soil was dirty in the eyes of the Lord.

Lord, pour anointing oil on the ground of this house
Father, Your power is mightier than a level-ten hurricane.
My Father loathes wickedness in holy places.

Heavenly Father, thank You for anointing and annihilating
the evil around my sanctuary.
My house is pure and consecrated in Christ.

My Lord, fill the outside of this house with Your divine
presence.
Your divine presence makes fallen angles quiver in hades.
Your strength surrounds my house like a fortress.

The kingdom of God dwells within and around my house.
My home is at peace because of the Almighty's presence.
Your presence, Father, puts peace in my spirit.

The blood of Jesus covers my house.
My house is beginning a new journey with my Father.
The hand of the Lord is upon this house.
The power of God and angelic beings surround this
holy place.

My house is holy.
Holiness and power of the Father terminates all wickedness.
The power of God within me has cast all evil into the pit
of hell.

Evil that steps foot on the ground of this house will be
burned by the blood of Jesus.
Many people will not return to my home,
for the Father has carried away those
demoniacs into the lake
of fire.

The lake of fire has consumed all the wickedness around
this house.
The Father had to destroy the first house in order to purify
this house.
The old house had to die so the Lord could do a new thing.

This house is at rest.
My house is restored to holiness and wholeness.
God and the angels surround my house like warriors on fire.

God's fire surrounds His people.
The Father surrounds His children
with His fire because of His
unconditional love.
This fire removes all fear and evil.

The fallen angels that surrounded this house are burning in
torment.
God's warrior angels are servants to God's chosen ones.
The angels of God rescue the Father's children.

My house is strong in the Lord.
My house has a dynamic presence of the Lord.
This house is set upon holiness.
Your holiness is beautiful, Lord.

My house will ravage all demonic possession.
Demoniacs will flee because of the anointing around this
house.
This house is standing firm on the Word of God.

The Word of God will annihilate all wickedness.
The Word of God breaks hindrances and barriers.
All hell may break loose, but the Word of God stands
forever.

Epic 20

I have been born into a family of animosity and
turmoil.
My ancestors, who were born in Trinidad, were
cursed.
Cursed is my family for generations and generations
to come.

The spirits of sorcery, witchcraft, and curses have
covered my mother and me like fleas stick to
a dead corpse.
The Prince of Darkness have commanded these
spirits to attack me for centuries.

Before the Creator formed the seas and sea monsters,
Satan had attacked me before I was formed in my
mother's womb.
These curses have tormented my body since youth.

The unjust judge is working through a voodoo priestess.
This voodoo doctor has evoked a sickness that man
cannot find.
This voodoo queen has cursed the righteous for centuries.

The fallen angels of Satan have terrorized my body with
evil.
These curses originated in the time of Sodom and
Gomorrah.
These curses from the pit of hell have wreaked havoc
on my life.

The voodoo priestess evoked the spirit of death upon my
life during my days as an infant.
The curse of death haunted me in mother's womb.
The spirit of death hunted for my health.

Curses and vexations have hovered over my son.
These evil spirits have thrown darts of malice at
our souls.
Our souls were once in bondage to the curses and
to witchcraft.

Psychics have collaborated with the underground for
my demise.
These false prophets have vexed my spirit.
These ungodly creatures have sent forth curses of
sickness and disease on a woman of God.

The genie spirit that is part of the fallen angels
is a mighty spirit and weapon in Satan's army.
The genie spirit has wreaked torment on many families.

The genie spirit wanders among nations.
This demonic spirit causes other demons to put curses
upon the righteous.

The unjust judge has curses in the pit of hell assigned
to God's children.
These enchantments have possessed the feeble.
Human flesh and ability are inferior to the power of
curses.

Many devils have stepped in my house and cursed my being.
Curses have been upon me from the time the Lord brought me into human form.

Many curses have been sent toward my unborn son.
The Father is fighting on His son's behalf.
The Almighty is hovering around my unborn son the way a father protects his son.

I am redeemed from the curse of the law.
The Father has removed all vexations from my body and mind.
The Father is a shield to those who take refuge in Him.

Heavenly Father, thank You for casting the curses in the pit of hell.
My Father will exterminate Satan and his fallen angels like never before.
The ghouls in hades are trembling because of the Almighty's power.

The Father is leading a revolution on behalf of those done unjustly.
This revolution will leave a mark for centuries to come.
Satan's weaponry and curses will be destroyed in the blink of an eye.

I am the apple of my Father's eye.
I am a diamond in the rough.
I am a precious gemstone in the eyes of my Father.

The Father is hiding me in His secret place.
The secret place is His heart.
Wickedness is but a millennium away from
the Father's heart.
I will abide under the shadow of the Almighty
for eternity.

My spirit and the Father's spirit are harmonious.
I am joined with my Father on earth and heaven.
I am surrounded by the Almighty's presence.

I have a spiritual bond with my Father.
The pits of hell cannot break the powerful union
between the Almighty and me.
The Holy of Holies has rescued me from the
vexations of Lucifer.

Satan's reign is soon coming to an end.
Curses, witchcraft, and sorcery are returning to
terrorize the witchdoctor.
The spirit and soul of the witchdoctor will be
judged by the Almighty.

These curses are going to invade the witchdoctors
like never before.
These vexations will torment the mind and body of
the voodoo priestess.
The enchantments will cover the bodies, souls, and
spirits of the witchdoctors.

The Lord is avenging His children's pain like never before.
Recompense and restoration are coming to the body of Christ.

In these last days, the Father will haunt and terrorize the spirits of sorcery, witchcraft, and curses.
The Father will torment Satan's own evil spirits.
God will cause His Spirit to haunt Satan after his death.

Epic 21

Heavenly Father, my spirit and soul cry in distress
and agony.
The inner man is being weakened by the trials and
tribulations of life.
Evil spirits are after the happiness and well-being of
my life.

My enemies glorify in the downfall of a mighty woman
of God.
Satan's family glorifies in my afflictions and persecutions.
The unjust judge has launched a mighty stronghold on
my spirit and soul.

I am weak in flesh.
My walk with Christ is becoming frail.
My heart is filled with anger and agony.
My soul is holding on for dear life to the Father.

I must endure the hardships of life as a warrior of God,
a journey that is tumultuous.
Young in age I may be, but the trials of life have weakened
my soul.

My enemies rejoice in my tears of sadness, and distraught,
I am alone in the wilderness of terror.
The spirits of melancholy, mourning, and anger hover
over my body.

The strongholds of Satan have latched onto me like a deadly pestilence.
The spirit of pestilence hungers for my divine health.
Divine healing is what I am determined to get.

My body, spirit, and mind grow weary in times of turmoil.
The unjust judge sends messages of death to my mind.
My mind is constantly battling the words of my Father and the voice of the adversary.

My body and soul are being crushed by the feet of the adversary.
I am weak in human ability.
Human strength is incapable of defeating Satan.
The fallen angels are magnifying my hurts and pitfalls.
Lucifer is evoking his army to destroy the call on my life.
The life of a servant of God endures persecutions and hardships like never before.

A servant of God must put on the whole armor of God to quench the fiery darts of the Wicked One.
Satan and his ghouls are planning pitfalls for my downfall.
Downfalls are temporary, but the rising of the Almighty's presence within me is eternal.

The underworld is sending the spirit of pity upon my being.
My family chuckles at the weakening of my inner man.
Though my spirit man is becoming faint, the Father is reenergizing it with power.

The abuse of life tarnishes the body of Christ.
Test and trials have enslaved me from peace and happiness.
The trials of life are obstacles from the pit of hell.

The spirits of pain, hurt, and agony are blocking me from
my God-given destiny.
My enemies stand and wait for me to be defeated.
The spirit of defeat lurks for my strength and confidence
in the Creator.

Though I may be struck down and tortured in human flesh,
I will not be destroyed.
I may have one last breath, but the Word of God stands
forever.

The adversary may have me chained with affliction and
iniquities,
but the Word of God is never chained or imprisoned.
The words of my Father are in my heart.

Life can throw a million darts at my flesh,
but my spirit will never cease to exist because my Father
and I are one.

Epic 22

I have roamed the streets of Sodom and Gomorrah.
I was once an ungodly creature who glorified in
Satan's riches.
I was a woman desolate and destitute.

Satan was the ruler and provider of my life.
I was an ungodly woman who solicited poisons
to the creatures of the night.
My greed and stubbornness kept me enclosed with the
unjust judge.

The Lord punished me because of my transgressions.
Money, jewels, and riches were driving my spirit to
gluttony.
Gluttony hovered over my spirit like devils clinging to
uncleanness.

My treasures were stored in Satan's kingdom.
The ungodly creatures of night hunted me for poisonous
substances.

These poisonous substances drove me into despair.
This poison wreaked havoc on my being.
These chemicals from the adversary vexed my inner being.

The chemicals brought forth treasures for my heart's desires.
The attire was a façade covering deep hurts.
My attire wore me.

I was a prisoner in Satan's kingdom.
The spirits of fear and anxiety overtook my mind, body,
and soul.
These strongholds roamed my house like a lion seeking
its prey.
I was enslaved mentally and spiritually to the unjust judge.

Through endless days and nights,
darkness clothed me like a woman of the night.
My spirit dwelled in darkness and torment.

My face was covered with shame and strife.
The wicked spirits clung to me like hunters on their
prey.
The spirit of torment clothed my entire being.

The spirit of suicide lurked the streets for my soul.
This spirit embedded thoughts of destruction.
This unclean spirit resided within the mind of a
chained prisoner.

Years and years of destructive thoughts drove me.
Though I walked in the flesh, my spirit was dead.
My spirit and soul died from the torture and torment
of the adversary.

Walking through the cities, the spirits of unhappiness
and torment would cover my heart.
Satan and his army drove daggers of agony into my heart.
He raped my life.

I was the walking dead.
Internally, I had bruises, lacerations, and scars
from abuse from the unjust judge.
Lucifer left marks of mental torment and torture.

My treasures were in deadly riches.
My treasures were invaluable and unclean in the Lord's
eyes.
Where a man's heart is, so is his treasure.

In the midnight hour, I cried, "Jesus, save me from my
adversary!"
The Lord grabbed me with His mighty hand,
And tears of happiness and joy covered the Almighty's
feet.
The eyes of the Lord are toward the righteous and His
ears are open to their cry.

The Creator has forgiven me of all my sins.
I am washed in the blood of the Lamb.
I am a new creature in Christ. Old things have passed
away; behold, all things are become new.

Father God, thank You for removing the dark spirit.
The Father had to consume my old spirit with fire so
the new spirit would be in the light.
The spirit of the Lord shines forth around my soul.
I am my Father's daughter and His queen.
I am a precious ruby and pure in the Almighty's
eyes.
My hands are pure with holy water, and I lift my
hands in praise.

Your mercy and loving-kindness endures forever.
The Father has saturated my heart with pure
unconditional love.
The love I have for the Creator is immeasurable.

The Holy One of Israel has anointed me with the
oil of joy.
The anointing on my life covers me like a shield.
The Father has crowned me with everlasting favor.

I am God's shining star.
It pleases the Father to see the light within my spirit.
The Father has blessed me with a light so bright that
all darkness must go in the name of Jesus.

I have a power within from the Father that will
destroy all wickedness.
I am my Father's chosen vessel and leader.
Christ has anointed me to preach the good news.

The divine presence of God saturates my inner man.
The Father is calling me to new levels in His presence.
The Holy of Holies is preparing me for battle.

My Father will come forth like a powerful wind.
His breath will pour out fire upon ungodly nations.

Epic 23

The Almighty's Spirit is like that of an eagle.
The eagle flies high and sees above all creatures.
The Mighty One's Spirit soars through the skies like
a powerful wind.

Father God, bless with the spirit of an eagle.
The eagle symbolizes power, honor, valor, and integrity.
Heavenly Father, grant me strong wings so I may
soar over the devils.

My Father has given me wings of brass.
These powerful wings will destroy the traps Satan
has set for me.
I have the spirit of a warrior eagle.

The Father has instilled an abundance of power within
my spirit.
The power of God will rise from within and overtake
Satan's kingdom.

My Father's Spirit and mine are combined on earth and
in heaven.
The Father has blessed with the power of an eagle.
The eagle is God's anointed creature.

The Mighty One in battle and I will soar through the
heavens.
The Creator's wings are dynamic in strength and power.
His wings are the color of snow and glow from His glory.

The Father's wings shelter those who fear Him.
God's wings, enormous in size, cover the righteous.
God's wings cover His face from the wicked and perverse.

Many godly nations are protected by the Father's wings.
The nations of the underworld run into the darkness at
the presence of the Lord.
Whatever is done in darkness must come to light.

Wings of power, might, and honor surround me like a
a medieval knight surrounding the king.
My Father in heaven has wings that stretch as far as
the Nile River.
God's wings are surrounded by the fire from His
lips.

Heavenly Father, consume my spirit and soul with
fire.
Cleanse my heart from all impurities with Your
dynamic fire.
Hide me within Your feathers; hide Your servant
under Your wings of righteousness.

There are many hidden treasures and secrets under
my Father's wings:
Secrets that are stored for the righteous, and
treasures where man nor beast can find.
Store your treasures in heaven where moths cannot
destroy them.

The jackals of the night try to ease their way under
the Mighty One's wing.
The jackals hide in dark places.
The jackals cover themselves with clothes of evil.

The jackals put on a face like God's angels.
These unclean spirits latch onto the righteous for
secrets.
These ungodly creatures hide in the caves of Satan's
kingdom.

The jackals and devils hide in places that are not
perceivable to the naked eye.
One must use discernment and spiritual eyes to call
them out.
The Father must shed His love in your spirit to defeat
these inhumane creatures.

Oh, how long will you, O devil of the night, hide?
How long will the jackal hide himself from the Creator?
The Father will hunt the devils and jackals like a vicious
wolf attacking its prey.

The demons of the night run to the ends of the universe.
The Father's eyes are looking to and fro.
The King of Glory's Spirit is moving over the places of
the wicked.

Darkness and light cannot be friends.
The darkness hides mischief and destruction
from the world,
but the Father sees and knows everything.

The Father's Spirit will demolish all evil in wicked
places.
My Father will crush all devils and jackals with His
mighty hand.
The King of Kings will destroy ungodly lands and
territories to wipe out the jackals.

Satan and his army are hiding in secrecy.
Hiding in secrecy is temporary.
Once the Father finds these devils, the hyenas of
the night will feed on their rotten souls.

He know what is in the darkness, and light dwells
with Him.
A man who hides from God is enslaved to darkness.
The wicked can only hide for so long.
The Lord exposes the wicked, and there He will
command the serpent and it shall bite them (Amos 9:3).

The day of the Lord is near many nations.
Devils, demons, and wickedness will be held accountable.
The God of Abraham will come forth like a hurricane
that eyes or ears have not seen or heard.

The evil done to God's people is being restored.
Every wicked being will flee from the divine presence
of Jesus Christ.
Wicked beings will be no more.

The Father is returning for His people.
The Lord will set His people on high.
The chosen people of God will soar with the Father
like never before.

Epic 24

In a loud, distraught voice, I cry, "Abba Father!
El Shaddai! Your daughter is crying in her spirit.
Heavenly Father, my spirit and soul want to
break from the abuse of sorcery and witchcraft."

The spirit of Jezebel has commanded divinations
and enchantments to surround a woman of God.
Endless nights of crying and distress surround my
mortal body.
The spirits of shame and terror hover over the house
of a warrior of God.

Fear, condemnation, and shame try to ease their way
into my inner being.
Thoughts of suicide and harming God's unborn prince
terrorize me.
My spirit and soul quiver at the thoughts in my natural
mind.

Dark images surround the windows and doors of my
residence.
Unhappiness, uneasiness, anger, fear, and worry lurk
the hallways.
The house of God is clothed in confusion.

Insomnia howls for my spirit man.
The spirit of insomnia tries to keep me from
hearing the Father.
The voice of the Father is mellow and calming.
The voice of Satan is loud and boisterous.

My spirit and flesh are at war.
Spirit and flesh cannot harmonize together.
The Creator distrusts the flesh because of its
indulgence in wicked things.

The carnal mind wants to give up.
The spiritual mind supplies godly wisdom and revelation
to the spirit.
God's awesome Spirit within me propels me to stand
and fight the good fight of faith.

I am at war with fallen angles.
Ungodly creatures are digging pits for my destruction.
Satan at every angle is throwing massive darts at
my flesh.

Your daughter's arms are weary from fighting.
My arms feel weak and feeble from the adversary's
obstacles.
Storms from the north, south, east, and west have
damaged my physical being.

The unjust judge is stripping me of confidence in the
Mighty One.
Satan has stripped me of the armor of God.
The Father's armor is hidden by fallen angels.

Satan has warped and distorted my vision.
My natural eyes are in terror of what will happen next.
The human eyes have believed the lies of Satan.

The eyes of a seer know God's angels surround me
like knights protecting their queen.
A seer from within is filled with the divine presence
of the Father.
My spiritual eyes have seen the downfall of Satan's
kingdom.

Though tears may try to drown a warrior of God,
the Lord will grab His servant with a mighty hand.
Tears of shame may try to cover my soul,
but when the righteous cry for help, His ears are open
to their cry.

Tongues of slander, condemnation, and betrayal are
aiming at my spirit.
Wicked tongues are wagging against a true servant of God.
But every tongue speaking against me shall be put to shame.
The Lord of Hosts says" My people shall never be put
to shame" (Joel 2: 27)

The Father is close to those of a broken heart.
Though my natural heart may be in agony,
my spiritual heart will never be crushed.

I am my Father's daughter.
I am not afraid of man or beast,
for the Lord has given the spirit of power, love,
and of a sound mind.
Soft-spoken, gentle, and meek I may be,
but the King of Glory has given me the spirit of
a giant and a conqueror.
All conquerors in Christ Jesus will leave a legacy
that shall be carried for millennia to come.

Epic 25

I have begun a new and awesome journey with my
Father.
The Creator of heaven and earth has drawn my spirit
before the foundation of the world.
My spirit and the Almighty One have a bond that no
devil can destroy.

The cross that God has assigned me is massive in size.
In the natural, my eyes and human strength cannot
bear the weight of this cross.
But the Lord has injected the spirit of might into my
inner being.

I have endured physical pain and emotional hurt from
my youth.
The spirits of loneliness and melancholy linger around
my soul.
My soul is in distress from the fiery darts of the wicked.

The spirits of fear and terror lurk the hallways of my
dormitory.
Fear is thirsting for my soul and spirit.

The spirit of torment hides in the darkness waiting for
my downfall.
In the midnight hour, my eyelids quarrel about staying
awake.
Though I may be terrified to close my eyes,
the angels of God surround the daughter of the King.

The adversary inputs thoughts of loneliness.
Satan and his army has sent forth ungodly young men
to lust after my soul.
The unjust judge has evoked the spirit of lust to hunt
for my purity.

The Devil has fallen angels disguised as godly men.
These lustful animals wear attire of a human but curse
the Holy One in secrecy.
These demons of the night indulge in promiscuous acts
like never before.

Satan has put on a façade to lure me into unclean
activities.
The adversary smiles as if he were compassionate,
yet Lucifer lurks around my innocence and
purity.

O Holy One of Israel, remove the scales from Your
daughter's eyes.
Father God, open the eyes of Your servant.
My Lord, bless me with a spirit of discernment so
I may know who is in Christ and who is a wolf.

Heavenly Father, shine forth Your bright light upon
my spirit.
My spirit is craving knowledge of the Father.
The King of Glory pours water on thirsting ground.

Take me into Your bosom, O Lord.
Reveal to the inner man Your divine secrets of
Your Word.
He reveals the deep and secret things.
The Holy of Holies has hidden treasures for His
children.

Turbulence and wars are en route to destroy my faith.
People will glorify at the trials and tribulations I must
endure.
Daggers and knives will be aimed to destroy a mighty
woman of God.

The Pharisees collaborate on my downfall.
Satan has caused many storms to rock my boat.
The mighty winds and heavy rainstorms try to pull
my spirit into the place of the dead.
The Lord my God will not allow His servant to drown
in the bloody river of hades.

The Devil is throwing curve balls with thoughts of
fornication, lust, inferiority, anger, lack, and suicide.
These unclean thoughts try to ease their way into my
prayer life.
The spirits from hell are pulling on my soul.

Though my flesh may desire the touch of a man
and intimacy,
though my flesh may give into temptation and
my flesh and heart may fail, God is the Rock
and strength of my heart and my portion forever.

Ungodly creatures are after my consecration and
purification in Christ.
Poisoned words try to fill my spirit.
When I cry, "Abba Father!" the Lord will hide me
under His wing.
Many evils confront the righteous, but the Lord
delivers him out of them all.

The spirit of death awaits my soul.
Death is like a vulture seeking a feeble man.
Death is trying to terminate my existence.

I plead the blood of Jesus on death.
Death has no say on my departure or my future
generations to come.
The Father has given me power over death.

I am one of God's chosen people.
I am a warrior in Christ Jesus.
The spirit of death is under my feet.

Church folk and others believe I have a cowardly
spirit.
Others say I am gullible.
Naiveté will no longer be part of my aura.

Christ has instilled within me an overflow of power,
strength, might, and revelation that is no match for Satan.
My Father and I are one.
My feet have walked on ground that other people have
yearned to see.

The vision of who I am in Christ is priceless.
The Father will breathe life and power upon my
dead spirit.
The King of Kings is breathing life into dead spirits.

My spirit is rising to new levels of power.
I am from the tribe of Judah.
I am descendant of Abraham.

I am from a bloodline of warriors: Christ, Abraham,
Isaac, Jacob, Joseph, and David.
I have my ancestors' power and strength in
my spirit.
God has summoned my ancestors' might into
my soul.

As I go from nation to nation,
the Father will cause my mouth to open, and
His Spirit within me will breathe fire upon many
nations.

Epic 26

Abba Father, save me from the hand of the
adversary.
The adversary has put traps in the path of a warrior
in Christ Jesus.
Satan hides in the shadow of darkness, plotting
wicked acts for my destruction.

Though I am a baby in my walk with the Lord, my
spirit is wise in the revelation of God's Word.
The elders of the church believe I am an infant in
the Word of God,
but my Father has instilled within me wisdom, glory,
and honor that overshadows my being.

The Creator of the universe has blessed me with power
that will shake the nations to come.
Many nations I have stepped foot on will bow and
give reverence to the Mighty One.
These nations will see deliverance, healing, and restoration
of sight through the hands of God's daughter.

The Holy Spirit is creating a fire within my soul.
My soul is hungering for a manifestation of the
King's power.
My Father has engulfed my spirit and soul with
dynamic power.

The Holy One of Israel has engrafted Himself with
my flesh and spirit.
My footsteps are embedded on the streets of Samaria.
I have a divine and supernatural presence that will
awaken the people of Jerusalem.

The people of Jerusalem are hungry for my
Father's Word.
Israel is crying for the return of the Lord.
The Lord of Lords is sending His anointed vessel
to spread the good news.

The people of Israel are embedded in my heart.
Children of Samaria will touch my hand and feel the
presence of El Shaddai.
Jehovah is leading many nations where people dare
to walk.

Ungodly nations are collaborating against a ministry
that God has ordained before my existence.
The Sovereign Ruler has instilled a ministry in my
soul that Satan cannot destroy.
My Father's ministry and I will conquer ungodly nations.

Wicked tongues are slandering me for my obedience to
the Father.
These evil tongues are filled with poisonous words.
These demonic people are evoking spirits of defamation
and slander.

The spirits of defamation and slander await in the darkness
for my demise.
Evil people are arising in the kingdom of darkness.
These wolves of the night hide in the forest, waiting for
my downfall.

Eyes the color of blood watch me as I go to and from
church.
These demons clothe themselves with the wickedness of
night.
Terror and fear roam the school hallways for my divine
scent.

The sweet scent of perfume surrounds my pure soul.
The presence of God is sweet like roses and tulips
blossoming on a summer day.
A sense of peace and joy surround a warrior of God.

The ungodly creatures of the night know the scent of
God's servant.
These devils leave traces of blood in the dormitories
to embed fear in my heart.
The blood of Jesus is against all evil in wicked
places.

The Enemy has covered my dorm room with blood.
The inscriptions on the wall say, "Defeat, anger, poverty,
lust, and suicide."
Demonic spirits have tried to attach these evil
words into the mind of a godly woman.

I have the mind of Christ and do hold the thoughts,
feelings, and purposes of His heart.
I bring every thought captive to the obedience of
Christ the Messiah, the Anointed One.
I command the angels of God's army to chain these
unclean spirits in Jesus' name.

The spirits of fear and terror try to overtake my flesh.
The Spirit of God dominates my flesh.
I am not lusting after the flesh or lusting with my eyes.

The Holy Spirit has ignited strength and power into my
soul.
My inner man is being stirred by the Father.
The Father's mighty hand is upon my life.

O Lord, my omnipotent God, lighten my path with
Your bright Spirit.
My Father in heaven holds the keys to heaven and hell.
Many will get thrown into the lake of fire for leading
God's people astray.

Tongues of the wicked will be removed from the mouths
of demons.
My Father will toss these devils to the ends of the
earth.
God's anger is rising against those who harm His servants.

Boils, tumors, leprosy, and deadly pestilence will cover the
evil like never before.
The day of judgment is near.
Woe to you who hide in darkness from the Almighty!

My Father, in His chariot of fire, is returning for His
children.
Restoration is but a few days away.
The Lord my God has restored me seven times for my
pain.

Pain and agony shall cover my family no more.
God's glory and might shines on our faces.
As I look into the heaven, my Father is smiling at my
mother and me.

Heaven is but a few days away.
My existence with the King in heaven is for eternity.

Soon our hands and faces will touch.
Soon I will be sitting at Your feet, my Lord.
Your are returning for me in the midnight hour.

My spirit is in heaven with the Father.
I am smiling upon my descendants to come.

Epic 27

Satan has vexed my body with pestilence, and sickness has overtaken my soul.
My soul and spirit are damaged from the wounds of abuse.
The spirits of abuse, sorcery, and witchcraft have lingered around my inner man.

Fallen angels have tortured and tormented my existence since I was a youth.
The spirits of fear, torment, and anger lie on the sheets of my bed.
Death hovers over my bed, provoking me to terminate my existence.

As I walk through the streets, the spirit of torment awaits my presence.
As I lie in the basement of hell, the spirit of torture clothes me.
Lashes, scars, and bruises cover my face and body.

Dark shadows cover my human body.
God's light that once brightened my spirit has diminished into darkness.

The darkness hides my unclean spirit from the truth.
Lucifer has removed the Almighty's word from my heart and burned it with wickedness.

Wickedness clings to my soul like flies to a dead corpse.
Death hunts for my scent through the streets of Sodom
and Gomorrah.
The angel of death evokes evil beings to curse my existence.

My spirit despises any divine presence.
The divine presence of Jesus makes
the darkness surrounding
the inner man quiver.
The devils surround me like prison guards an inmate.

I am an inmate of the kingdom of darkness.
The ghouls of the night have infected my spirit man with
darkness.
I have disobeyed the Creator and have been caste into the
lake of fire.

The adversary and his army have rejoiced in my destruction.
Curses, witches, and evil beings have led me astray from
the light.
A hedge with knives, thorns, and thistles surround my body.

Bars surround the hedge so I cannot escape torment.
Chains, bars, and fire have embedded in my spirit.
I am enslaved to the unjust judge, along with tormenting
spirits.

Wicked female beings have confiscated my life.
My life has been surrendered to Jezebel.
Jezebel has chains hovering over my immortal spirit.

The spirit of Jezebel taunts me in the midnight hour.
Jezebel whispers evil poison into my feeble ears.
Her spirit controls the movement of my being.

Jezebel has evoked the spirits of witchcraft and sorcery
to mark boils on my body.
The boils on my body have weakened my appearance.
My eyelids grow heavy from the lashes and bruises of
the Wicked One.

Lucifer has caused a deadly parasite to feed on my flesh.
Parasitic creatures feed on my impure body.
The blood from my body drains into the mouths of the
ungodly creatures.

Ungodly creatures feed on my soul like cheetahs feasting
on a weary dear.
The animals of the night have drained my spirit and soul.
I am lying in a puddle of death and taunting.

My physical being is dying from the harsh abuse of the
adversary.
The adversary whips my soul with a belt of thorns, thistles,
and nails that has ripped my inner man.

My inner man is no longer whole but has holes from abuse.
Satan is trying to erase the inner man.
In the spirit realm, my soul is dark,
and I walk as a hunchback,
roaming in the darkness.
I have one last breath.
My spirit quarrels with Satan over my life.
The adversary's feet have crushed my immortal spirit
into the pit of destruction.

I am lost, Father God.
I cry aloud, saying, "Save Your son's last breath!"
Heavenly Father, reach from Your throne of grace
and save me with Your mighty hand.

My Lord, You said, "Repent and be baptized in the name
of Jesus for the remission of sin, and you shall receive
the gift of the Holy Ghost."

Abba Father, have mercy on my soul.
Forgive them for they know not what they do.
My Lord, crucify these demonic spirits in my life.

Consume my dead spirit with fire.
My Father, breathe life into my dead soul and restore
fellowship.
My spirit cries for restoration with my Father.

Take me home, Father.
Take me into Your bosom of unconditional love.
Shed Your love upon my unclean heart.

Your love is awesome, God.
"Perfect love casteth away all fear". (1 John 4:18)
Rejuvenate my spirit with love and strength.

Death has no say on my departure.
I have a journey to complete with my Father in heaven.
My purpose was ordained before the devils were
created.

God will raise my spirit from the place of the dead.
Satan must remove his hand from my life and my
Descendants' life in Jesus' name.
The angels of God will encamp around me.

I am like the prodigal son.
My Father is calling me.
I surrender all to the King of Kings.

This is the year of restoration.
God will restore all that has been lost.
The King of Glory has put a ring on my finger,
symbolizing a bond that no devil can destroy.

The same power that raised Jesus from the dead
can raise me!

Epic 28

My soul and spirit have been crushed and weakened
by the adversary.

The spirits of envy, jealousy, and hatred cover my face.
As I lie in bed distraught and distressed,
my eyes are heavy and weak from the attacks of Satan.
Tears of melancholy, sadness, fear, anger, and suicide
cover the feet of the Lord my God.

After endless nights of weeping,
my heart has been tarnished from the tumultuous times
of my life.
My spirit man cries aloud for cleansing from the Father
in heaven.

The Devil has marked my soul with bitterness and
resentment.
The spirits of bitterness and resentment hover over
my body
like a dark, murky cloud over the water of the Red Sea.

Lord, cleanse my soul in the Red Sea.
Heavenly Father, pull my soul from Satan's kingdom.
El Shaddai, toss all of the fallen angels from the
earth who are trying to tear my family apart.

Curses are aimed at my house from the pit of hell.
These demonic curses have caused strife between my sister
and me.
These generational curses have wreaked havoc on my family.

The God of Abraham, Isaac, and Jacob have called my sister
and me into a covenant before Satan was created.
The spirits of strife, anger, and animosity cover my house
like demons latching onto uncleanness.

The fallen angels roam the hallways and basement for my
weakness.
The unjust judge has evoked the spirits of heaviness and
weakness to keep my spirit in the dark.
These fallen angels have chained the inner man from the
truth of God's Word.

The Word of God never lies.
The almighty God will never leave you nor forsake
you.
The Creator will grab your dying spirit and breathe
His might and power into your mortal body.

In the midnight hour, evil thoughts have vexed my
mind.
Thoughts of harming myself have covered my unclean
mind.
Satan implements sadistic thoughts, trying to end
my existence.

The spirit of torture lurks my bedroom for my presence.
In my youth, I was tortured and punished by the
adversary.
The adversary caused my earthly father to bruise
my frail and fragile body.

The spirits of drunkenness and anger covered the house
in which I was born.
My earthly father bruised my spiritual heart.
My father would call me derogatory names.

As I looked out the window as a little girl,
the spirit of drugs would clothe my father's image
like dark shadows hovering over evil beings.
Satan would chase me through the house with his belt
of irons and nails.

My face and body were bruised from the lashes of a
drunken father.
Chaos, humiliation, and shame have covered me since I
was a youth.
In the midnight hour, I would cry, "Jesus, save me from the
hurts of my father."

Tears of blood would stream down my face because of
the torture I endured.
That little girl inside of me is ashamed because of the
demonic things my earthly father did.

My soul and spirit are dying from the torment of Satan.
Satan covers my house like crows lingering around, waiting
for death.
Death awaits in the darkness for my downfall.

Arrows, daggers, and swords aim at my mind.
Darkness hovers over my mind.
The darkness has warped my mind with distorted
images of myself.
Satan has crucified my soul from the Father's love.

Deep within my immortal soul, I know the King of
Glory loves His princess.
Shower me, O Lord, with Your loving-kindness and
tender mercies.
Father God, remove not your Holy Spirit from me.

Spread abroad Your unconditional love.
Remove all hatred with Your impeccable love.
The Creator's love is for everlasting eternity.

Restore fellowship with my sister.
O Holy One of Israel, You created a spiritual bond
between my sister and me that no devil in hell can destroy.
Draw me to Your Spirit, O Lord.

Consume my spirit with fire from the heavens.
Breathe Your Spirit upon my flesh.
My Lord, descend upon me the way the dove descended
upon Jesus.

Jesus, save me from the place of sheol.
Lord, remove the hedge that Satan has put around my
descendants.
God, remove all fallen angels from my house with
a powerful wind.

I have surrendered all to the Father.
Satan no longer has authority over my life.
I am filled with the Godhead, Father and Son.
The Son of God has wrapped me in His bosom.

I am seated on the throne with my Father.
The Father has anointed me with the oil of joy.
The King of Kings has turned my mourning into joy.

The Lord of Lords has cleansed me with holy water
and the baptism of Jesus.
I am pure in the eyes of the Lord.
I have done no wrong.

The Father has called me to walk with Him before I
was conceived in my mother's womb.
I am married to the Father.
I am conjoined with my Husband in spirit and on earth.

I am His wife, and He is my Husband.
My Husband is calling me to be at rest with Him.
I will dance with my Father in paradise for eternity.

Epic 29

Heavenly Father, pull my soul out of the wilderness
of confusion.
The spirit of doubt covers my aura like an obsessive
husband.
My Lord, as I lie in the bed of confusion and terror,
streams of tears flow down my face.

In the spirit realm, my tears are of blood.
The blood from my eyes symbolizes the trauma I
endured as an adolescent.
As a little girl, I would cry, "Jehovah, save me from the
hand of the adversary."

The spirits of chaos, terror, anger, and distress filled
the hallways of my house as a young girl.
Sorrow and melancholy lingered around my house
like rats hunting for dirtiness.
In the midnight hour, my spirit would be overwhelmed
from the beatings of Satan.

The adversary roams like a roaring lion, seeking who
he may devour.
As a youth, I observed Satan roaming the hallways
of my house.
The darkness of the night covered my face from the shame
and agony that came upon my family.

Generational curses from Africa have hunted my scent
as well as the Father's precious daughter, who I was carrying.
The demons of the night would cross the seas, evoking
sickness and enchantment on my fragile body.
A little girl who hid pain in her heart from the abuse of
Satan.

As the owl of the night whistles, the spirit of drunkenness
overshadowed my earthly father.
My earthly father terrorized my mother, and I engraved
anger in my heart toward men.
Screams of terror, hurt, distress, and agony lingered around
a house of God.

My earthly parents were at a tug-of-war between the Creator
and Satan.
My mother, strong in the Lord's Word,
My mother's heart was fixed, trusting in the Lord.
Deep in my mother's heart, she knew her husband
would surrender all to the Almighty One.

My earthly father was corrupt in his ways.
The Lord my God was displeased at how he was treating
His daughter.
The Father unleashed His wrath against
my father for the abuse.

O Lord, heal my heart from the wounds of my father.
The spirits of distrust, lack, and poverty came upon me like
lions seeking their prey.
I have allowed Satan to solicit me into heathen activities.

I have laid in the bed with ungodly creatures.
The ungodly creatures have touched my body with unclean
hands.
These unclean hands have left unwanted scents on my body.

The wolves' tongues and lips have kissed my unclean body.
The spirits of lust, sex, and perversion would haunt the
cities of the night for my soul.
My soul was dying from all the attacks of Satan.

Standing in front of the mirror, I would weep at the
ungodly things I have done.
In the mirror were images of the monsters that took pleasure
in my activities.
I have hid my face from El Shaddai long enough.

The spirits of shame, humiliation,
and defeat no longer control
my being.
The Father in heaven guides my footsteps into His divine
presence.

I have been cut off from the wicked men of the night.
The ghouls may try to flash their filthy money, but "my God
shall supply all [of my] needs according to His riches in glory
in Christ Jesus". (Philippians 4: 19).

The Messiah is calling me on an awesome journey.
The Father is holding His daughter's hand.
Though Satan has pitfalls for my destruction, God will
deliver me from the hand of the wicked.

O Holy One of Israel, wipe my tears of sadness with Your
hand of righteousness.
Tongues of the wicked are wagging, bringing up my past.
Satan wants me to live in the past.

But there is no condemnation to those
in Christ Jesus. (Romans 8: 1).
Every tongue that rises against me shall be put to shame.
The Lord says, "My people shall never
be put to shame. (Joel 2: 27).

The spirits of shame and humiliation will no longer terrorize
my future generations to come.
When the spirits of terror and fear see God's divine presence
around me, they will run because of the name Jesus Christ.

Christ dwells within my heart and my soul.
The Messiah and the angels are
protecting the Lord's princess.
Though I may not feel like praising in the natural,
my spirit is forever praising the Father in heaven.

As I look into the heavens, God shines His bright light upon
my face.
The Father's light and glory—oh, what a presence!
As I walk from nation to nation, the Father's light will be
embedded on the streets in the physical and spirit realm.

Epic 30

Heavenly Father, fill me with the fullness of joy and
happiness.
Lord, fill my heart and my stomach with Your Word.
The Word of God is precious and is engrafted with my
heart.

O Holy One of Israel, invade my mind with the sword.
The sword of God is sharper than any two-edged sword,
piercing between the division of soul
and spirit. (Hebrew 4: 12).

The carnal mind rejects the true Word of God.
But the spiritual mind is hungering and thirsting for the
knowledge of God.
Who is he that can find the knowledge in the Father's heart?

The Father's heart is pure and precious,
a heart that is as clear as a diamond in the rough.
All of God's children are embedded in His heart.

As I stand at the feet of the Creator,
He opens His majestic arms and saturates me with
unconditional love.
The love in Jesus' heart is far more precious than diamonds
and rubies.

Diamonds, rubies, emeralds, sapphires, and other beautiful
jewels are valuable in the natural.
But the love of the Father surpasses all wealth and jewels.
Wealth and jewels are temporal items,
But Abba Father's love is for eternity.

A wicked man in his heart believes luxurious possessions
are the key to happiness and prosperity.
As an ungodly man flourishes in the kingdom of darkness,
Satan has enslaved this man to the torture and torment of
wickedness.

An unsaved man flaunts his possessions to other folks.
The wicked men of the night steal treasures from
God's people in the spirit realm.
Wealth has been in the wrong hands for centuries.

After centuries, decades, years, months,
and days of hiding the
treasures from the children of Israel,
God's people are torn between God's provision and
remaining in bondage to Pharaoh.
Pharaoh has caused many demonic storms to assault the
children of God and steal their wealth.

A battle between God's people and fallen angels,
a battle between good and evil,
a battle between God and Satan.

The fallen angels have resisted God's people long enough.
Father has sent powerful angels to defeat the forces of
darkness.
The angels of God's army have ravaged Satan's kingdom.

The kingdom of Babylon is coming to an end.
Wars, storms, tornadoes, and other catastrophic events will
take place.
Ungodly nations will ravage one
another and enslave many in
the kingdom of darkness.

Ungodly nations are rising to oppose the government of God,
but the Spirit of the Lord is stronger than any legion.
The Almighty Lord will chase and haunt any dark force until
it is destroyed.

The King of Glory will never leave nor forsake His
children.
Storms, hurricanes, and the seas will try to overtake God's
people,
but the Lord has His mighty hand against wicked storms.

The Father in heaven has the authority to make raging
waters cease.
The Lord God has given us power to tread upon serpents
and scorpions and over the power of the Enemy.
Nothing shall by any means hurt us.

As the days go by, the time for Jesus' return is near.
Jesus is our high priest and my high tower, redeemer,
healer, and protector.
The Son of Man has called God's leaders to go into
this dark world and be a bright light to those in
darkness.

The forces of darkness have kept God's children from
their God-given destiny long enough.
God is instilling His children with boldness and courage
like never before.
The weak and cowardly will be bold as a lion.

Manifestations of the living God will be seen like never
before.
Christ is invading the earth with power.
The wicked will no longer have the power,
but the righteous shall inherit the earth.

The ungodly creatures will fall into their own pit of
corruption.
Curses, vexations, enchantments, sickness, and disease will
overshadow the wicked.
The Lord shall cut off strength from the wicked, and His
might shall increase the godly.

The evil will drown in their dirty and slothful ways.
The wicked shall suffer from the wrath of God.
The wrath of God will cause a deadly pestilence to come
upon the unjust.

The unjust will weep for God's mercy, and Jehovah will
hide His face because they did not accept Christ as the
living God.
The Holy of Holies has no mercy for evildoers.

The bodies of the evildoers will be tossed to and fro.
The leaders of ungodly nations will be buried, nowhere
to be found.

But those who wait and give their life to Christ will have eternal life.
Eternal salvation is more valuable than any evil deed.
All evildoers will endure torment, torture, and the burning of their souls and spirits for eternity.

Epic 31

God's children are crying in the spirit for the Lord's glory.
The Lord's glory is so heavy that my spirit cannot handle its power.
The power within the Father is so dynamic that demons tremble in their spirits.

Unclean spirits of the night wander the filthy streets in search of uncleanness and weakness.
The ghouls of the underworld have somehow crept into the homes of God's people.
The body of Christ is defeated due to a lack of knowledge.

Abba Father's infinite wisdom and knowledge keeps God's people from being attacked.
Fiery darts are aimed at the soul and spirit like never before.
The seven "ites" are overtaking some of God's people.

The Canaanites are creeping their way into the souls of the saints.
The spirits of inferiority, lack, poverty, and anger are hunting for faith.
But we have been born into a family of warriors.

The Almighty One has crucified and consumed the previous
spirit with fire.
The fire that breathes from the Spirit of the Lord consumes
and destroys all unrighteousness.
All darkness and uncleanness must go in the name of Jesus.

Christ has redeemed His people from the curse of the law.
Light and darkness cannot dwell together.
So why are God's children still in darkness?

Why are God's people serving both masters?
Two masters cannot be served.
You will hate one and love the other.
"You cannot serve both God and mammon". (Matthew 6: 24)

Some spirits are dressed in sheep and appear
to be God-fearing.
Under the disguise is a ravenous wolf that
desires true followers of Christ.
The sheep appears to take on the characteristics
of a human,
but the spirits despise and curse the living God
in secrecy.

False prophets are now roaming the streets like never
before.
False prophecies and lies are aimed at God's people.
The children of God are suffering because they
trusted in a lie.

The Lord's eyes are watching our every move.
The ungodly are hiding in places where mankind
cannot go.
But the Lord will expose these false prophets and so-
called healers very soon.

The Lord knows what is in darkness, and the light dwells
within Him.
The saints have been put to shame, humiliation,
and embarrassment and taken advantage of long enough.
The kingdom of God is invading dark places and earth
like never before.
Plots from the wicked, collaborate against the saved,
stealing their health and secret traps will be brought
into the light.

The wicked have been running and hiding long enough.
The fallen angels have been corrupting the just for
too long.
Curses, vexations, and enchantment will overtake the
witches and warlocks like never before.

The curses, vexations, and enchantments will terrorize
and haunt the wicked.
The wicked will drown in their blood.
Innocent bloodshed will be avenged by the King of Glory.

Unjust acts are recorded in the mind of God.
The Father is angry with the wicked.
The Father in heaven will no longer hold His peace.

The time for justice and recompense is here.
The Master sees and knows His children are crying
and hurting.
But El Shaddai is invading the earth with a strong
downpour of blessings.

Things stolen from the body of Christ will be returned.
God will haunt and torment evildoers until payday.
The unjust will have sleepless nights.

Every wicked act and hateful crime will be judged by the
Holy One of Israel.
The wrath of God can annihilate any planet within the
blink of an eye.

The Father's anger is so ferocious that the wicked will
want to jump in the lake of fire.
God is releasing His anger on the unjust.

Pestilence, disease, infirmities, and curses will drown the
spirits of the wicked.
The wicked laugh at the righteous suffering unjustly.
But the Lord will open His mouth and cause a devastating
calamity to come upon the wicked.

The unjust despise the just.
Evil loathes good deeds.
The accuser chuckles at the righteous in their downfall.
But the Holy of Holies is looking down from His holy
habitation in heaven and saving His children from the
hands of the adversary.

As Satan snickers in the darkness,
the Lord is sending out warriors to bring demonic worlds
to nonexistence.
The Father has an army that can destroy one thousand men
in one second.

The world will be no more.
Satan's reign will cease to exist in the matter of a second.
No more hardship and suffering; only peace in paradise,
soothing waters, and calm winds.
Another world, another life—a new life—in the kingdom
of God.

On streets of gold and silver,
the Father is teaching His children righteousness
and peace in the spirit and in heaven.

As I close my eyes, the Father says, "Welcome home,
daughter. Job well done! You have completed
your assignment!"

Epic 32

The blood of Jesus saturates my mind, soul, spirit,
and body.
The adversary cannot evoke spirits or pestilence upon
my descendants and me because of the blood of the Lamb.
As I plead the blood of Jesus upon myself and future
descendants, the fallen angels run and quiver in the cave
of darkness.

The darkness of the night covers the earth like insects on a
rotten corpse.
I am in a dark, murky world filled with hatred, anger,
suicide, deception, and other wicked things.
But Christ within illuminates my spirit and soul so I
may walk among wolves.

I am a sheep walking among wolves.
As I walk through the wilderness, the wolves growl and
hiss.
Disturbing noises, frightening images, and distractions try
to taint my walk with Christ.

Though I am dressed in sheep's clothing, my spirit is as
bold as a lion.
As I tread upon places with the Father, His Spirit illuminates
my being, driving away all evil.
The evildoers try to hide in places where humans would
dare to go.

My Father has anointed me to spread the gospel to every living creature.
My words are spirit, and they are life.
The almighty God has blessed me with a mouth to speak things into the earth.

The earth is cursed and desolate,
but the living Christ has redeemed me from the curse of the law.
Jesus has been made a curse so I could be made righteous with the Father and have eternal life.

O Lord, if I could have a glimpse of eternal life.
Treasure chests filled with coins and God's will for His children guarded by warrior angels.

As I look up, the Father carries me away in His bosom.
El Shaddai's heart is massive and strong yet compassionate and loving.
The Father's wings are enormous and heavy, embroidered with diamonds.

The Father has wrapped me in His majestic wings.
As Elohim covers me with His warring feathers, the demons run into their caves.
As the wicked plot my demise, the Lord has hidden me in the secret place.

Take me to that secret place, Lord.
Take me to that place where I can be with You forever.
Take me from a world of evil and plant me in heaven.

O Lord, heal my broken heart.
You are close to those of broken heart.
Father God, rescue me from all the fiery darts.

The adversary chuckles in the pit of darkness.
The adversary awaits my downfall as he sends storms
and hurricanes to sink my ship.
The Holy One of Israel will not let my spirit drown in
sorrow and misery.

Though Satan is sending bullets to my mind and soul,
the Almighty One has wrapped me in His powerful
feathers.
The Father's wings are so enormous that He soars the
skies and evil flees from His presence.

I have a divine presence that surrounds me like angels
encamped around the Father.
I am seated in heavenly places with the Father.
The Father has sent me to heal the brokenhearted and
set the captives free.

Lord, as You look down from Your holy habitation in
heaven, burn my flesh with Your fiery eyes, and
crucify my flesh so I can be more like Christ.
Flesh and spirit cannot dwell together.

Nail my flesh to the cross, Lord.
Take my spirit, Lord, to heaven.
Burn the old spirit with ravaging fire;
engulf me, God, with Your flames.

I am surrounded by fire from the Father.
As the devils throw knives, the fire from the
Father cremates any wickedness.
Though Satan tries to turn up the heat in the
fiery furnace,
My spirit and soul can never be burned.

The Father has put a hedge around His servant.
His servant cannot be touched.
I am hidden in the secret place.

Satan tries to throw weapons of destruction,
but the Lord has hidden me under His wing.
Rocks, thorns, and thistles are thrown at God's
wings,
but the Father crushes all evil with a swoop of
His wing.

The Lord has His eyes set upon His children.
But those who do harm to the righteous will
be burned in their souls.

Epic 33

O God in heaven, why must I suffer?
Heavenly Father, take me home.
I am weakened by the adversary's stones.

I am longing to be in my Father's arms.
Why must the wicked flourish?
Evil creatures of the night curse and speak
blasphemy against God's people.

Ungodly creatures chuckle at my pain.
The devils are placing bets on my downfall
and destruction.
These devils are hiding in places that are invisible
to the naked eye.

But God Almighty will hunt down the filthiness
of the unclean spirits and expose them.
He knows what is in the darkness, and the light
dwells within Him.
All darkness and evil must go when the Almighty
speaks.

Lightning and thundering in the heavens at the Holy of
Holies and God's angel armies prepare for battle.
The Father's armor is embroidered with diamonds
and contains a sword so long that once it penetrates
the spirit, the spirit will die.

Satan is calling forth his legion to destroy mankind.
But when Abba Father walks onto the battlefield, His
steps are so powerful that demons will cry.
No man, spirit, devil, or beast can withstand the
Master's power.

Yahweh is returning for His people.
Every sickness, vexation, curse, and wicked thing done
to me will be judged on judgment day.

Master, avenge Your people of the adversary.
Your children are crying for an outpouring of God's
manifestation.
Healing the sick, deliverance, and freedom will be
manifested like never before.

Lord Jesus, You died so I could be made righteous
in the Father's sight.
You have called me before I was formed in my
mother's womb.

My flesh is scared of what will come to pass.
But the God of Abraham will save me from the hand
of Satan.
No more will I be bruised and crushed by the hand of
Satan.

Though daggers and knives are piercing my body
and causing grief,
the Lord my God has put a hedge around His servant.

Though I go through rugged waters and demonic storms,
the Father has given me a sword to defeat any sickness
and any devil.

Satan is razing me like never before.
The adversary has a dug a pit of destruction for my
downfall.
Hidden traps are set for a mighty woman of God.

I am rising to new levels of power, might, and wisdom.
The Father is within me.
The Lord will cause me to triumph in many dark areas.

Evildoers and haters of the Word of God laugh at my
sorrow.
Woe unto you who laugh at a servant of the Lord.
But when the Father rises and exalts His servant, the
wicked will crumble in their destructive ways.

Abba Father, breathe a deadly pestilence upon the
wicked.
Open Your mouth, Lord, and burn the ungodly with a
fire that is for eternity.

I despise the wicked and their loathsome ways.
Master, damage the souls and spirits of the wicked.
Throw the spirits of the wicked to and fro where they
will never be found.

All those who rise against me will be brought to their
knees by the Holy of Holies.
I will not be defeated in my walk with the Father.
I will not fall into the lake of fire.

Though Satan tries to push me further away from my
calling,
Jehovah-Jireh has me locked in His mighty hand.
Crush Satan, O Lord, with a mighty blow.

In the natural, Satan is undefeatable.
But in the spirit, Satan is as weak and vulnerable
as a helpless goat.
Satan, you are defeated, for my God and Jesus
reign.

The time will come when God will judge His people
and Satan's people.
Satan's army will be defeated and extinct for all
eternity.
But my Father and I will reign in heaven.
I will be at peace in my Father's house.

No more crying, no more sorrow and sickness.
No more stonings, beatings, and crucifixions.
I will stand at the Father's feet, and my spirit will
ascend into heaven.

Epic 34

The Lord is my strong, high tower and
the portion of my life forever.
O Lord, I am running for dear life.
As a young boy, the spirits of gloom, sadness, terror,
and suicide have surrounded me like a prisoner.

The Enemy has put a hedge of destruction, torment,
and anger around my family and me.
From the moment my ancestors stepped foot in
America,
the adversary had planned a destructive and
chaotic life for my family.

The unjust judge, before my kinsman and I were
formed in a fleshly body, devised schemes to destroy
my family and me.
Generations and generations of strife in my family.
Why do You allow Satan to torment me?

Since my youth, Satan has had a mighty grip on my
family and our lives.
Many unclean spirits are running through generations
of my family.
As the years progress into darkness, the fallen angels
grow mightier in my family.

Abba Father, what iniquity was caused in my family?
Jehovah, why have You allowed so much torture to
come upon my kinsman and me?
O Lord, why have curses, vexations, and bewitchment
covered the souls of my family?

Abba Father, Your son is growing weary in the battle
against Satan and his army.
Seven nations that are mightier in spirit are increasing
in strength.
The strong man has a grip on my descendants' and my
lives.

O Holy One of Israel, we must bind the strong man!
Father, breathe Your Spirit into my weak and decaying
Spirit.

Show a sign, O God, of Your goodness so my
enemies may be put to shame.
Bring down the arrogant and the haughty, El Shaddai,
so they will know I am God's son!

The ungodly chuckle in the darkness about my downfall.
Fallen angels have evoked spells, curses, and sorcery to
weaken my faith.
Wicked beings are rising against me to terminate my
existence.

Yahweh, I cannot fight these mightier nations in my
strength.
My soul and spirit are crying in distress.
The adversary and his fallen angels have crushed my
inner being.

I am like a dead corpse floating down the river of destruction.
Satan has commanded the tide of the sea to pull me farther away from God's truth.

The adversary has blown a demonic storm in my direction.
My spirit is crying for mercy and help.
Lord Jesus, my boat is sinking into the sea of destruction.

The adversary haunts and hunts the unclean streets for my scent.
Satan and his angels track the footprints of God's servant.
My scent is of the Lord, like the blossoming of roses on a sweet summer day.
The adversary's scent is that of a burning, rotten corpse.

The unjust judge is a spirit that is foul and detestable in the nostrils of the Father.
Boils, tumors, infirmities, iniquities, pestilence, and filth cover Satan.
Satan and his fallen angels try to hover over me with their loathsome spirits.

Though I may be thrown into the fiery furnace,
though Satan is trying to increase the intensity of the fire to burn my inner man,
the almighty God will cover me with His mighty wings.

In the flesh, stones, rocks, and thorns are weakening my mortal body,
but the spirit man is undefeatable.
I have a power within me that will make Satan and his demons quiver in their sleep.

The Father has given me power to tread upon serpents and
and scorpions and over all the power of the Enemy.
Nothing shall by any means hurt me. (Luke 10: 19).
I am at peace with my heavenly Father.
For we must not wrestle against flesh blood, but against
principalities of darkness and spiritual wickedness in
high places. (Ephesians 6: 12).

No demon in hell can tear the Father from me.
My Father and I are one.
I am created in God's image.
I am a replica of the Lord my God.

Though Satan may cause disastrous storms,
I, too, can cause the winds to obey me.
I have a storm within me that will ravage ungodly nations.

Satan has just awakened a sleeping giant.
People may look and think I am a weak, uneducated,
low-class person,
but eyes and ears have not seen or heard that God is raising
a new generation of radical warriors.

I am like a tree firmly planted by the streams of water.
I am a warrior clothed with the armor of God always
protecting my mind and spirit form the ravenous wolf.

Satan walks around like a roaring lion, seeking who he
may devour. (1 Peter 5: 8).
But the Father has given me the sword, the Word of God, to
destroy Satan.

No devil, beast, man, or Satan can remove the sword of
God from my spirit.
Any devil that tries to take the sword from heart will be
smitten and burned by the hand of the Lord.

Looks are deceiving,
but the Lord searches the heart and the mind.
Though my eyes and physical appearance look
weary,
My heart and soul are on fire for the living God.

I am a true testament to God's Word.
Even though I am mocked for serving Christ,
the Lord will cause my enemies to bless me.

Though I appear to be of low status,
I am rich in God's Word.
The Lord will open up the windows of heaven,
pouring out blessing until there is
no room to receive. (Malachi 3: 10).

Woe to you who laugh at a true follower of God!
As you have done, so shall it be done to you.
Your dealings will return upon your own head.

Any ungodly creatures who cursed my family and me
will reap what they have sown.
The curses will hunt the wicked, and the wicked cannot
hide.
Even unto the darkest place of the world, the curses will
find the wicked, overtake the spirits of torment, and
torture them in their minds.

Hell will burn their loathsome spirits as they cry and scream for water.

But I will be in paradise with my Father, and the wicked will reach for mercy.

But the Lord will say, "If I ascend into heaven, thou are there: If I make my bed in hell, behold, thou art there". (Psalms 139: 8).

Epic 35

O Holy One of Israel, I feel so alone and distant from
You.
Why do You allow Your servant to be punished by
the adversary?
I am walking in a dark, murky world among
uncivilized and demonic beings.

The adversary's kingdom grows mightier in these
last days.
The end times will be filed with strife, turmoil, demonic
possession, pestilence, and disease as these unclean
and foul spirits lurk the streets.

Lord Jesus, I fear for the lives of people who do not
know the living God.
The Son of God is crying aloud for purification in the
body of Christ.
Jesus is weeping tears of melancholy because of the evil
of the world.

The heart of Jesus is hurt and saddened because of unbelief
in Christ.
The heart of Christ weeps because many people will be
burning in hades.
Hades is a kingdom of darkness filled with the souls and
spirits of evildoers.
The whoremongers, fearful, sorcerers, and witches will
burn in the lake of fire. (Revelations 21: 8).

The lake of fire will consume the unbelievers and the evildoers in their souls and spirits.
The smell of burning corpses of lust, fornication, adultery, idolatry, and rape will fill hell.
Hades is filled with murders, rapists, pedophiles, and and other wicked creatures.

Many unbelievers and the wicked will suffer at the hand of Satan.
The unclean spirits from the underworld try to crawl up for mercy and a drink of water.
The unclean spirits reach for the hand of God for mercy and salvation.

What is cast down in the lake of fire cannot come into heaven.
Once the evildoer is cast into hell, that unclean spirit is a permanent slave to Satan.
Satan is the god of this world and the Prince of Darkness.

Satan is raising up more witches, sorcerers, magicians, and other wicked beings.
Many people will be deceived by the works of Satan.
Healings, miracles, signs, and wonders will be taking place,
but it will not be the Lord my God who manifests these wicked acts.

Many false prophets roam the cities to and fro, prophesying false prophecies.
These false prophets are driven by demon possession.
These fallen angels will capture the hearts of many with their deceitful lies.

The unjust judge is pulling the curtain over many peoples eyes.
Many will be led astray by false teaching and doctrine.
People will no longer live by sound doctrine but by man's knowledge.

Many believe his ways are righteous and virtuous.
Mankind tries to eliminate the God factor.
Mad scientists are trying to replace the Creator of heaven with scientific theories.

The steps of a good man are directed
by the Lord. (Psalms 37: 23).
The Lord holds His servant's life and cherishes it with unconditional love.
The love of the Lord is so powerful that it drives out all evil.

The almighty God is returning with a vengeance.
"'Vengeance is mine' says the Lord.
'Do not avenge yourselves, for vengeance
is mine". (Romans 12: 19).

The Lord is my avenger, vindicator, and strong, high tower.
He is my refuge and my fortress, my God.
In Him will I trust.
In the time of need or trouble, the Lord will save me from the hand of the adversary.

Jehovah's eyes are roaming to and fro the earth.
The Lord has His eyes on every person who has
done His children wrong.
My Master keeps records of every wrong thing done
by the wicked.

Hot coals from the Father's lips will be breathed upon
the heads of the wicked.
But the Antichrist will deceive many people.
The Antichrist will demonstrate signs, wonders, and
miracles to the world.

False prophets are beginning to rise in this dark,
murky world.
But the true prophets and true servants of the Lord
my God shall reign for eternity and cast these
false teachers into the depths of hell.
Satan has lured God's prophets into the kingdom of
darkness.

These demonic prophets are filled with spirits of evil,
deceit, wickedness, and lies.
These prophets of Satan roam the streets to and fro,
seeking unbelievers who will follow them to the
pits of hell.

Satan's prophets speak with an eloquence that
saturate the mind and the spirit of the unbeliever.
The eyes of the unbeliever will be amazed at the signs
and wonders of these false prophets.
These false prophets appear to be sent from God.
Only the spirit of discernment can identify a true prophet.

A true prophet comes with peace and joy in the name of
Jesus.
A prophet of the Lord knows the thoughts of the person
with whom they are communicating.
True prophets have boldness and confidence in Christ
Jesus.

A prophet of Jehovah sees into the spirit of that person.
The prophet of God opens his or her spiritual eyes to
any hidden devils.
Fallen angels are hiding in areas of darkness that
are invisible to the naked eye.

But Abba Father is raising prophets with spiritual
eyes that will expose these devils.
These fallen angels chuckle in the darkness,
but the Lord's eyes are roaming to and fro.
He knows what is in the darkness, and the light
dwells within Him.

The Spirit of the Lord is moving across the Red Sea.
The Spirit of Jesus is hovering over the entire universe.
The universe moves at the hand of almighty God.

God has the universe in the palm of His hands.
The Father blows a mighty wind to keep the planets
and the universe turning.
But soon every living thing must cease to exist.

As the sun and the moon collide,
the moon will turn red and the earth will shake and
crumble.

Stars and galaxies will collide and burst into flames.
Fire from the depths of hell will ravish the souls and
flesh of the unbelieving.
Burning flesh and corpses will rot in the cities of the
underworld.

Those who keep the Lord's commandments will have
everlasting life.
The fallen angels will climb the walls of hell to escape
torment,
but the Father will put a seal over hades so no wicked
thing can look out or try to climb from the lake of fire.

I will be with the Father in heaven, rejoicing and knowing
that my family and I are ready.
The Lord will erase every bad memory so I can be at
rest with Him.

Epic 36

In the midst of turmoil and trial, the Lord is
working on my behalf.
I know the almighty God is working behind the
scenes.
I walk by faith and not by sight.

Satan may try to throw darts and arrows of mass
destruction,
but the Father has put a hedge around my spirit man.
Though the outer man is decaying, the inner man grows
increasingly strong.

I wear the whole armor of God.
No devil in hell or demon can withstand the tornado
that God has put in me.
I have a hurricane in me that will make demons
quiver in their sleep.

As I walk through the dark forest, the fallen angels
hiss and gnarl.
The fallen angels are throwing fiery darts and curveballs
at my head.

The fallen angels growl as I get closer to my God-given
destiny.
Satan has pitfalls set up for my destruction so I may
fall into the pit of hell.
Though Satan has traps set for my demise, the almighty
God will keep my feet from being pulled into the
underworld.

The underworld is filled with sickness, pestilence, boils,
tumors, voodoo priests, and witches.
The witches of the underworld are collaborating with the
wicked on earth.
The devils of the night send people who appear to
be God-fearing but wreak havoc on the just.

The Almighty's presence is everywhere.
Those who collaborate against the just are doomed for
eternal torment.
Satan is the author of torment and torture.
The spirits of torture roam the unclean streets for
centuries.

Many unclean spirits roam the world for its victims,
but the Lord is in His chariot of fire, avenging His
children.
Within the blink of an eye, the Father can cause a
calamity.

The Father knows the heart of man.
The heart is deceitfully wicked and cannot be trusted.
Out of the abundance of the heart the mouth speaks.

Jehovah, look through our souls and hearts with Your
piercing, fiery eyes.
The Father looks deep within the soul and searches the
heart and mind for ulterior motives.
There are many ulterior motives in the body of Christ.

The body of Christ is at war.
The goddess of war has summoned the demons of the
underworld to overtake the minds and spirits of Christ's
disciples.

Though we may be in a dark, murky world filled with
pestilence and disease,
the darkness of this world will not and shall not
overshadow the power of God within my soul.
God's bright light illuminates my spirit in a cruel,
demonic world.

The spirit of Jezebel haunts and hunts the streets for a
prey.
Jezebel is a whore who manipulates the soul into
lustful acts of perversion.
Her spirit is foul and detestable in the nostrils of the
Father.

O Lord, put a hedge of protection around Your servant.
There is a war between good and evil.
The day of Armageddon and the opening of the seven
seals is but days away.

The Father's army and Satan's army are preparing for
battle.
Abba Father and Satan are battling for supremacy.
Lucifer is clever, witty, and cunning, but has no strength.
God Almighty in His omniscience causes the
winds, seas, and oceans to collide with space.
Planets, galaxies, glaciers, and stars collide when God
breathes His Spirit upon them.

Jesus has the universe in the palm of His hand.
God causes the earth to rotate about the sun.
The sun, oh, how it warms and soothes the body.

The omnipotent God, the Creator of heaven and earth,
wisdom and might are His.
No other gods can compare to the wisdom, strength, and
power of the Father.

Icarus flew close to the sun and was burned.
The ungodly and the spirit of gluttony try to climb high
into God's temple to steal, wisdom, wealth, and jewels.
But the Lord my God has godly wisdom stored for
the righteous.
The righteous are never forsaken.

The followers of Satan desire to be in darkness and filth.
Hell is filled with many detestable and diabolical spirits.
Satan's fallen angels latch onto the souls of these unclean
foul beasts and feed on their souls and spirits.

But those who steal from the children of God will be
tortured in their souls.
The devils will feed on and drain them of their spirits.
The lake of fire will consume any foul being.

Some will fall by the hand of Satan.
Satan has his hands on his followers and is leading
them into a deeper and darker path of destruction.
Destruction, gluttony, anger, hatred, and deceit
shall cover Satan's foul and detestable spirit.

Sickness did not originate in the garden with Adam.
God has come back to restore the garden of Eden on
Earth.
Heaven is invading the earth.

We are moving into a time when God's people will rule
the earth like kings and queens.
Many will function far beyond their natural abilities.
Our brains will function like Jesus'.

Jesus is manifesting His presence more and more.
The Father's children will be like a walking god,
bringing life to desolate and ruined places.

The omnipotent God will manifest His presence
in a powerful way.
Eyes and ears have not seen or heard that God is going
to hit the earth hard with His glory.

God's people will be covered with gold.
People's hair will turn from gray to black
God's people will take the earth
From Satan and will have dominion over it.

Look out, Satan, because God's children are coming with
the sword, the Word of God.
The Father will bring wrath upon Satan and the
unjust that will torture them for eternity.

Epic 37

The Lord my God will avenge me of my
adversary.
The Holy of Holies has a plan for my life.
Though I wallow in self-pity and distress, the
almighty God will breathe His awesome Spirit
into my spirit.

I was a demonic man.
I would hide my face in the darkness from all
cleanness.
The legions fed upon my flesh like vultures
devouring a human.

The spirits of torture and torment followed my
spirit wherever my foot stepped.
I was enslaved to the demonic powers and
satanic forces.

My eyes grew dark, murky, dull, and possessed
with evil and hatred.
My eyes were the color of red.
Red symbolizes that my soul was immersed with
evil and possession.

I would howl and cry out in the midnight hour.
My roar was that of a ravenous lion.
I would growl like a demonic wolf, seeking all
flesh to devour it.

Claws of hot iron would claw my unclean
flesh.
I hid my face in silence from the Father.
The Father was calling me to be cleansed.

Though bats and vampires were feeding on my
soul,
the Father swooped from His chariots of fire and
with His mighty majestic hand cast those ungodly
creatures into the pit of hell.

I am not myself, Lord.
You, O Lord, did not create me to be a deranged
demoniac.
Your created me to be at peace with my heavenly Father.

The spirits of darkness are trying to attack my mind,
soul, and spirit.
The spirit man is weakened from all the evil that was
within me.

Burn my spirit, O God, for the unclean spirits are
trying to take possession of my soul.
The spirits of torment, fear, torture, and suicide has
me bound in chains.
O Lord, break the chains of possession and curses.

Abba Father, cast the curses and divinations into the
pit of hell.
My mind is traumatized and filled with evil.
Satan has control over my mind and has evoked
powerful devils to control me.

My soul and spirit are bruised and scarred from the
iron rod.
My hands and feet are chained to the pit of hell.
Satan has a whip with spikes, and the spikes have
crucified my inner man.

I am drowning in darkness.
The ungodly creatures feed on my soul and spirit
so I cannot fight.
My body is evaporating in hades.

I am numb from the abuse of Satan.
I can no longer feel my spirit or soul.
My soul cries aloud in agony and distress.
I am screaming and crying, saying, "Lucifer, stop
abusing me!"

No one hears my agony and distress.
No one knows that I am dying from mental and
physical abuse.
The mental and physical abuse caused by the adversary
has traumatized my spirit.

The adversary is having a party for my downfall along
with my soul perishing.
The devils are blowing trumpets and horns about
my defeat.
Satan chuckles in the darkness as I crawl into
the light.

As I crawl to the Father, the devils try to block
me from receiving eternal life.
But God Almighty stomps the pillars, and the demons
are cast to the uttermost parts of the earth.

The earth is filled with wicked beings.
But these wicked beings shall be no more,
for the Lord my God will torment the devils in hell.

God, the Creator of heaven and earth,
the omnipotent Spirit of God, is in dark and
light places.
But the light dwells within Him and drives out all evil.

Evil is no match for the Creator.
The Creator has wisdom, might, power, and knowledge
that no beast can withstand,
for the mark of the beast is no match for God
Whose power no foe can withstand.

The day is near when God will resurrect my soul.
What was meant for harm, God will use for my good.
The spirits of insanity, witchcraft, torture, torment, and
suicide were meant for my harm.

Had the Lord not allowed me to die, I would not have
been able to see the light.
My old spirit and soul must be torched with fire from
heaven so I can be clean in the eyes of the Father.

Crucify my spirit and soul, O Lord.
Cleansing me with fire is the best thing that has
happened to me.
The Father knew what was in my spirit and soul.

Christ looked past my flaws and saw that my spiritual
heart cried for Him.
The Lord God Almighty knew that one day He was
going to resurrect my spirit from the dead.

My spirit had to die so I could be made righteous with
the Father in heaven.

Our old previous mortal spiritual condition must pass
away before we can sit at the Father's feet.
The Father's throne is surrounded by the elders and
warring angels.
The angels hearken to the Word of God.

I am seated with the Father in heaven.
I have done no wrong.
My spirit is pure in the eyes of the Lord.

Though my flesh and heart may fail, the Lord will
not cast me off, for He is my portion forever.
My spirit and soul had to be burned of all impurities.

I am a new creature in Christ.
Old things have passed away; behold, all things are new.
I had to die a brutal death to have everlasting life.

I am crucified with Christ. Nevertheless I live, but
yet not I, but Christ liveth in me;
life in which I now live in the flesh of the Son of God,
who loves me and gave Himself for me.

Epic 38

The Lord my God is calling me to a deep
understanding of Him.
The Lord is gracious, slow to anger, and His
loving-kindness and tender mercy endures forever.
The Lord my God will never remove His
unconditional love.

Though I may have murdered, stolen, and destroyed
the lives of innocent people,
Christ, who liveth in me, has cleansed me in the
blood of the Lamb.
The blood of Jesus is so dynamic that it purges all
unrighteousness and uncleanness.

As I walk through this dark, demonic, murky world,
my Father has me in His heart.
Jesus has placed a hedge of protection around His servant.

The Lord's mighty Spirit hovers over the entire universe.
God's eyes are roaming to and fro the earth.

The Almighty One has the universe, stars, cosmos,
galaxies, and people in the palm of His hand.
Jehovah causes the stars, galaxies, and the earth to
be calm.
The planets, cosmos, and shooting stars move
upon the Father's command.

Power, fire, and wisdom surround Abba Father's throne.
As the Father speaks forth His omnipotent wisdom,
fire spreads through the heavens and the earth.
The Father's words are power-filled!

No demon, Satan, witchcraft, sorcery, or legion can
withstand the ferocious words of God.
Jehovah's words make demons and Satan quiver in
their filthy spirits.

The Father is a bright Spirit in dark, crooked places.
The Father's Spirit can drive out demons the moment
His presence is manifested.
Demons and Satan run into darkness as Christ steps forth.

God always masters evil.
Wicked ways, deceit, lying, and the shedding of innocent
blood is foul in the nostrils of Elohim.
The Father's heart is grieved because of so much
evil.

Jesus is praying continuously on the saints' behalf.
Christ is interceding for many nations and people
at the Father's throne.
Jesus is weeping for mankind.

Humans are lost in the darkness.
Satan has caused people to be blinded by fallacies,
but the truth of God's Word never lies.
Abba Father's word does not lie, for God cannot
lie.

The Creator holds fast to His promises.
The moment God speaks, whatever He says shall
be done.
Once God speaks, His words become law.

God is the judge, lawgiver, and king over heaven
and earth.
Whatever is bound on earth will be bound in heaven,
and whatever is loosed on earth will be loosed in
heaven.
God's words are law, and His government shall never
change.

There is no democracy in heaven.
God is the ruler and king over every human and
creeping thing.
It is the Father who keeps the animals and the solar
systems under control.

Before the foundation of the world, God had spoken
things into existence.
The earth, animals, humans, and skyscrapers were
not formed from nothing,
for the Father had spoken these creations before they
manifested.

Words have tremendous power.
Words can destroy or transform chaos into good.
Life and death are in the power of the tongue.
Those who love it, shall eat its fruit.

Guard your heart at all times, for out of it springs
the issues of life. (Proverbs 4: 23).
God's people must allow good things to shape
their hearts.
The Word of God is the only tool that can uproot
wickedness.
Evil shall never prevail, for the Lord has His hand
against those who do evil in His sight.

The Creator sees and knows everything.
The Lord knows our thoughts and words before we
speak them.
The Lord searches the heart and the mind of man.

The Father knows our hidden abilities, talents, and
motives.
The Master knows our prayers and supplications
before we ask.
The Father has an answer for every problem under heaven.

Hidden mysteries and answers are stored for the
righteous.
The prayers of a righteous man availeth much. (James 5: 16).
If your heart is wicked and unclean before the
Lord, your desires shall not be granted.

The heart is desperately wicked and deceitful.
God does not trust our flesh,
but he looks at the heart of man.

Being made righteous through the blood of Jesus is
why were are able to come boldly before the throne
of God.
Before receiving Jesus as Lord and Savior,
our spirits and souls were foul in the presence of God.

Now that we have been purged by the blood of Jesus,
we are able to stand in the presence of God, free from
all uncleanness.

Saints of God, the Father has given us something special:
His only begotten Son.
Children of God, love and surrender
wholeheartedly to Christ.

Brethren, I count not myself to apprehend, but this one
thing I do, forgetting those things which are behind
and reaching for those which are before me;
I press toward the mark for the prize of the high
calling of God in Christ Jesus. (Philippians 3: 14).

Epic 39

Times of great distress and turmoil are coming.
The devils of the night will be possessing and
feeding on the ungodly.
The ungodly try to set traps for the righteous, but
in the end, the wicked will fall into their own pit of
destruction.

The wicked flaunt their money and arrogant ways.
The ungodly boast about their wealth and education.
The evildoers look down on the poor and righteous.

The wicked chuckles as the body of Christ endures
hardships.
Satan and his fallen angles hide in the darkness, throwing
balls of destruction.
The evildoers hide their filthy faces from the day.

The wicked hide in darkness.
The ungodly creatures hide in places that are not
sensed in the natural.
Demons have certain territories that are run by legions.

Satan's army has people imprisoned in the spirit.
Satan has caused the fallen angels to evoke sickness,
disease, pestilence, death, and vexations to come upon
people.
The world is covered with darkness and deception.

The fall of Adam has caused the ground to be cursed.
The earth will be cursed until the return of Christ.
But the body of Christ has been redeemed from the
curse of the law.

Satan wants people to be in bondage.
Satan wants Bibles out of schools and God eliminated
from everything.
The adversary has covered people's eyes with deception.

The adversary walks around like a roaring lion seeking
whomever he may devour. (1 Peter 5: 8).
The adversary's voice is boisterous and loud.
The Father's voice is calming and soothing
to the spirit.
Satan has a grip on many people.

There is a strong man behind every demonic spirit.
The strong man has chained people in the spirit.
There are evil legions surrounding people in the
spirit.

Before you go into the strong man's house, you
must first bind the strong man.
One cannot defeat a legion of devils in the flesh.
One must call upon the Lord to defeat Satan's army.

Satan's army may appear to be mighty in the natural
realm,
but in the spirit, the angels of God's army will
exterminate a legion of devils.
Devils flee from the presence of the Lord.

The presence of the Lord is supreme over any wicked
force.
The forces of darkness are no match for God's wrath.
Beast, man, or devil cannot withstand the power of the
living God.

When the Father speaks, His words make devils tremble
and flee.
Devils even bow at the name of Jesus.
The Devil despises the Lord Jesus Christ.

Light and darkness cannot be roommates.
Light and darkness despise one another.
But the illumination of Jehovah's Spirit drives out
all darkness.

The Father's Spirit will always wipe out darkness.
What is done in the dark shall be manifested in the light.
Things are only hidden temporarily as a means for
revelation.

For there is nothing hidden except to be revealed;
anything temporarily kept secret is so it may be known.

All evildoers will soon find out that the Lord has His
eyes on everyone.
Anyone who does evil in the sight of the Lord will be
punished severely.

The haughty and proud will be brought down.
God will cause the wicked to fall from their horses.
The wicked will no longer occupy positions of high status.

Abba Father is going to eradicate this worldly
government and invade the world with the kingdom
of God.
The ungodly will soon be exposed as the ravenous
wolves they are.

The Father is going to reveal to the seers and prophets
the inner man of the ungodly.
The wicked will soon drown in their pity after exposure.

The wicked will try to hide their faces after being put
to shame.
The evildoers will turn the gun on themselves.
The Father will hide Himself from the evildoers and
cause demons to destroy them.

The wicked will weep for clemency on the day of
judgment.
The ungodly will want forgiveness,
but they had turned their faces from the Lord and did
evil in His sight.

You, O Evil One, have tried to lead God's people astray and
opposed them.
But the Almighty One will cause the demons to overtake
the ungodly.

The wicked will suffer harsh and brutal attacks in hell.
The fire of hell will burn away at the minds and spirits of
the wicked as they yell for clemency.
If I make my bed in heaven, the Lord will be there,
if I make my bed in hell, the Lord will
be there. (Psalms 139: 8).
Hell is made for Satan and his fallen angels.

Anyone who is a follower of Satan must lie in the bed of
torment for eternity;
screams of torture and torment in hell for eternity.
God's people, at rest with the Father.
No more weeping, pain, or distress in heaven.

The smell of rotten, burning spirits in hell.
The devils will feed on impure souls.
Laughter and joy in heaven.
You choose life or death.
I pray that you choose life.

Epic 40

We are not against flesh and blood but
against spiritual wickedness in high places—
the rulers of this dark world and every high thing
that exalts itself against the true knowledge
of God. (Ephesians 6: 12).

Brethren, be mindful that in these last days, people
will try to lead you astray.
People who are dressed in sheep's clothing may appear
to be Christ like,
but inside, a ravenous wolf seeks to devour.

Be of a sober mind and vigilant because the Devil,
who walks around like a roaring lion, seeks who he
may devour.
But the eyes of the Lord are toward the righteous and
hears their cry. (Psalms 34: 15).
Satan is no match for the wrath that lies in the Father's
Spirit.

Satan you are defeated, for my God and Jesus reign.
Christ, who is the head of the church,
our sovereign and omnipotent God, has defeated Satan
before the foundation of the world.

Be not afraid, my child, to walk into dark places.
Be not afraid to walk into your God-given destiny.
Before you were born, the Father injected Himself
into your spirit.

Jehovah has ordained me to preach the good news.
The Lord will send me to ungodly nations to set the
captives free and heal the oppressed.
The Father's Spirit is in every nation.

The almighty God is raising warriors and generals in
Jesus' name.
In the last days, the Father's army will be dynamic in
defeating the forces of darkness.
God's people will be at war until the return of Jesus.

The Father has given us a deadly weapon—a sword,
the Word of God.
The words of God will eradicate any demonic
force.
Satan knows who you are.

The fallen angels know you by name.
The moment you entered the world, the fallen angels
collaborated with one another for your demise.
The legions are structured in a way that the strong man
drives them.

The strong man advises his army on military strategies.
In the natural, Satan's army may appear to be lethal.
But the Master's army has weapons of mass destruction
that will blow Satan out of his boots.

The Enemy appears as a scary and grotesque image.
The Enemy's voice is bullying, trying to make God's
people speak against their heavenly Father.
But the inner man is flowing outwardly, causing Satan
to flee.

Lord, why dost thou allow Satan to torment the minds of
people?
Lord, why does Satan set traps when he has been defeated?
The unjust ruler does not and will not abandon his mission
to exterminate God's people.

Though the Enemy may throw fiery
darts, thorns, and thistles,
though Satan may try to throw us in the fiery furnace,
the gates of hell will not prevail against God's chosen people.

I have been thrown into the web of sickness.
As I was trying to escape the demonic web, the Enemy
evoked the spirits of pestilence upon my body.
Running from pestilence was not an option.

The Lord had to break that curse.
God destroyed the web and breathed life into my decaying
spirit.
I crawled out from under and climbed
over the wall of despair.

The darkness tried to keep me enslaved to pestilence,
but the living God shined forth His bright light and all
pestilence broke away from my spirit.

Light and darkness cannot be friends.
The darkness tries to keep us from the truth.
Satan wanted me to believe that God is my enemy.

The Lord is a strong tower, an advocate, and a refuge to those in need.
Our God never leaves His people in distress.
He will never you leave nor forsake you.

The flesh cries in pain and agony during adversity.
Our souls feel like they are being burned by the fires of hell.
Though we may be nailed to the cross, our spirits live on with the Father indefinitely.

Epic 41

The Lord Jesus Christ will return like a thief
in the night.
Mankind does not know the time or the season
of Abba Father's return.
Mankind tries to rationalize in its futile mind
the return of Christ.

There are many false prophets and teachers wandering
in the world.
These false prophets and teachers give the people
false hope.
They whisper lies filled with deceit and arrogance.

There are false spirits who utter deluded and heretical
doctrine.
The Lord my God shall not be made a mockery of,
for those who mock the Mighty One shall be thrown
into the lake of fire.

Beware of those who are dressed as sheep.
Though they may have scholarly knowledge of
Jehovah, in their corrupt hearts, they detest the Lord.

God is good for eternity.
There is no unrighteousness or lack in the Father's
kingdom.
The Father's kingdom is filled with treasuries, which
are for His saints.

Abba Father has a surplus of knowledge, wisdom, and
revelation.
There are hidden secrets and treasuries that the world
has no revelation of.
The Master hides His precious items so no wicked
thing may lay hold of it.

The Father will not withhold any good thing from His
people.
The Creator hides away sound and godly wisdom for
the righteous.
The righteous will never be without God's precious
wisdom.
Wisdom is far more valuable than gold
and silver (Proverbs 8:11)
One must have wisdom from the Father to keep Satan
under his feet.
One must have the revelation of the Anointed One
to ravish the kingdom of darkness.

We are in perilous times, times of distress.
Things will become hard to bear.
Those who sneer at the righteous enduring
adversity shall fall by their own sword.

The sword, which is the Word of God, will eradicate
all demonic forces.
There is no sickness or anything that is too difficult for
the almighty God.
Strength, might, and valor are contained in the Father's
Spirit.

The Lord my God has made His people in His image.
God can command the winds to obey His voice,
so the body of Christ can command storms to cease
because Christ has injected Himself into our spirits.

The body of Christ must learn to live through the
inner man.
Though our outwardly appearances are decaying day
by day, the inner man grows progressively stronger.

The Wicked One no longer has sovereignty over us.
Satan is powerless in the eyes of the Jehovah.
The Father has defeated Satan before the foundation
of the world.

Dear brethren, do not be alarmed or dismayed when
terror comes your way.
Do not be weakened in spirit by Satan's attacks.
Do not grow weary, for in due time you shall reap
reward if you faint not. (Galatians 6:9)

Satan's objective is to pull us down to his level.
The unjust judge constantly aims at pulling down
God's people.
God's people have been born from above and given
dominion over all things.

God's people have been redeemed from fear.
We have been redeemed from the curse of the law.

Saints, do not allow fear to take hold of you.
You are in the world but not of the world.
Fear does not tell God's people what to do.
We are warriors in Christ Jesus, and we tell fear
where to go!

The King of Kings has bestowed on us an
impeccable weapon—
the sword, the Word of God.
The sword is dynamic in strength and can pierce
through any situation.

My Father has injected His magnificent Spirit
into the inner man.
The inner man is as ferocious as a lion,
for I have the Spirit of my Father in heaven.

The Lord's people are on the move.
The Master's glory is going to hit the earth in
ways that mankind has not seen.
Fill the earth with Your glory, O Lord.

Give us a spiritual revival,
for we yearn the son and daughters of God
to be manifested.
We are hungry for Your return.

God's people will soon reign the earth.
What was once chaotic and desolate will be
brought back to order.
Waste and desolate places will see signs, wonders,
and miracles confirmed that Jesus is still Lord.

Jesus is alive!
Jesus is roaming the earth, seeking warriors who
will spread the good news.
Jesus is looking for radicals who fear what no man
has to say but rather fear the Lord.

The time will come when God's people will rule
like God.
We will be like giant gods, ravaging ungodly nations.
These nations will demonstrate by giving God's
people honor and reverence.

We are royalty and our King has seated us on high.
Boldness, confidence, and courage will overshadow
the righteous like never before.
Those who make a mockery of the righteous will
be brought to their knees,
for the Father has spiritual force that will make the
cosmos and stars collide.

Though perilous times are ahead, know that God's
servants have a force from within that can annihilate
a nation.
Jehovah is returning for His children in His chariots
of fire.

The people of God will be at peace in their souls and
spirits
while the wicked will be brought down by their own
sword of destruction.
Those who dig a pit of for the righteous shall fall into
the place of sheol.

Saints of God are promised peace and calm for eternity
while the ungodly man will seek answers.
But he will never find them because he is enslaved
to the darkness.

Epic 42

Lord, I am bruised internally, mentally, spiritually,
and emotionally.
As I lie on the bed of death, I contemplate my life.
From my youth, I have been tortured and traumatized
by Satan.

As a little girl, Satan sexually abused me.
The spirits of suicide, incest, sadness, and melancholy
clothed my soul.
The spirits of drugs and prostitution haunted the dark,
murky streets for my soul.

Satan has been after my soul since I was a youth.
The adversary caused my earthly father to defile me
in a way that no daughter should know her father.

Heavenly Father, I ask You, why do You allow Satan
to torment me?
O Lord, why have You allowed Satan to torment me
in my spirit?

A childhood filled with chaos and strife.
From my youth, Satan has planned a traumatic and dark
path for my life.
The spirits of darkness, weakness, melancholy, and drugs
have a hold on my soul.

Heavenly Father, my spirit wanders the streets of this demonic world.
Dark spirits are hovering over my weakened and abused soul.
As I close my eyes, dark spirits taunt me in my dreams.

Devils whisper evil, satanic, poisonous words in my ear.
Dark spirits are driving me into despair and suicide.
I am enslaved to the forces of darkness.

Physically, I am in the world, but mentally, spiritually, and emotionally, I am in a dark world.
These dark spirits have formed a strong man.
This strong man is being powered by many demons.

These demons have formed a mighty chain of other demons around my soul.
My eyes are heavy and gloomy from satanic attacks.
The adversary chuckles in the darkness of night.

The unjust judge has caused fiery darts to pierce my dark and weakened soul.
Fiery darts from hell burn my spirit as I scream for freedom.
My spirit is burning, O Lord. Help me!

Abba Father, keep my spirit alive so I may see my family.
O Lord, I want to look into the eyes of my loved ones.
I want to tell my son that I love him more than life itself.

But I must go to everlasting life with my Father.
The trials and tribulations of this world have brought
me to despair.
In heaven, there is no sorrow, crying, worrying, pain,
or sickness.
Sounds of laughter, music, and love fill heaven's
atmosphere.
The presence of the Father is mighty and intense.

Lord God, forgive me of my sins, for I know not what
I do.
O Lord, forgive those who have tortured and abused me.
Forgive them, Lord, for they know not what they do.

My death will not be in vain!
My spirit will live on for eternity in heaven!
My spirit will no longer suffer!

My dear son, words cannot express the love I have
for you.
Though I may have been driven by dark spirits,
El Shaddai knows that I have thought about you
endless nights, dear son.

Mother knows her precious son loves her.
You were formed by the Creator in my womb.
Before the foundation of the world, and before the
trees, plants, and the blossoming of rosemary tulips,
God called you to be my son.

Most dear son, your spirit is crying in agony and distress.
My son, do not weep for me, for I will be at home with
the Lord.
The angels of God cheer as I come home to the Father.

My Father has welcomed me home with open arms.
My Father treats me like His precious daughter.
I have been cleansed of all unrighteousness.

My old spirit has been consumed with fire.
Jesus, consume the spirit with fire.
Lord, You have a fire that can consume a nation.

Purge my spirit in the lake of fire.
The old spirit must be eradicated so I can be in the
Father's presence.
Uncleanness must be burned to be seated in heavenly
places.
I am a new creature in Christ. Behold, all things are
become new.

My spirit and soul are at peace with the Father.
I am singing hymns.
The Father has blessed me with a sweet yet powerful
voice.
My voice will be embedded in the hearts and minds of
men.

My son, remember the songs your mother has sung and
placed in your heart.
My son, I am at peace. Let not your heart be troubled,
for I am in paradise with the Creator.

My face is smiling upon you, my precious son.
As I look from the heavens, joy leaps from my heart,
knowing that God has His hand upon you.

My heart is no longer troubled,
for God has given me a new life in heaven
and a new spirit that is wrapped in the Father's heart.

My spirit and soul are weary from combat,
for though I am dead in the natural, my spirit lives
endlessly.
I had to die so the Lord could bring forth His
Spirit and image in His daughter.

Epic 43

O holy Lord, You are the God in whom I take
refuge.
You are the fortress and strong tower in which
I hide.
You are a shelter to those in need.

As I cry in distress, the Lord my God will hear my
tears in heaven and wipe them from my face.
I am lost in a world of confusion.
The spirits of confusion, anger, resentment, and defeat
howl the streets for my scent,
for the devils of the night know the scent and aroma of
God's people.

Times are getting difficult.
Ships of trouble, chaos, and turmoil are headed toward
the Lord's children.
These demonic ships are powered by the adversary.
The adversary has evoked fallen angels to steer these
wicked ships into the lives of God's consecrated people.

These nebulous and mystifying ships are planning attacks.
The ships of Satan are filled with wicked forces that nobody
can defeat in the natural.
Though Satan's army may appear to be robust and grand,
the Mighty One has an army with an infinite number of
warriors.

The God we serve is more dynamic than any force on
this earth.
Your Majesty, Creator of heaven and earth,
turn these evil ships around for Your people's sake.

Though I may be growing weary in flesh and blood,
the Lord has rejuvenated my spirit with fire.
The unjust judge is using his tactics to make me weary.
Satan is pounding my flesh to the ground.

Though Lucifer may appear as a robust spirit who
can do all things and tries to deceive others
by mimicking the Father,
the Father sees, knows, and hears everything.
Jehovah knows the thoughts and motives of all.
One may try to escape the Almighty's presence, but
His presence is even in the darkest places where man
would dare not go.

Satan has assembled many of the weak and fearful
into his camp.
The adversary has put a veil over many people's eyes,
deceiving them.
Woe to you who lead God's people astray!
God is unveiling false leaders, teachers, and prophets.

There are many false prophets wandering this opaque
world.
We are in the world but not of the world.
O God, those prophets who lead Your children astray,
slash their tongues so they may never prophesy in the
name of Jesus.

Be mindful to say, "Thus says the Lord!"
for flesh and spirit cannot harmonize together.
There is no good thing that dwells in the flesh.

O Lord, O God, allow Your Spirit to rest on those
who obey Your statutes.
Those who reverence You and honor You shall
have longevity.
God did not design His children to have a short and
mediocre life.

The Father has injected His awesome Spirit into our
spirits so we can live for eternity.
The spirit of death is a wicked tyrant.
Death is constantly hunting the streets for our souls.

Though death has confiscated the lives of God's people,
their deaths shall never be in vain.
When we die, our body returns to the dust, but our spirit
has passes over into paradise.
In paradise, there is no sorrow, sickness, or death, or hate.
Heaven's atmosphere is filled with the Father's
unconditional love.

The spirit of death may appear to be stronger
and have the final word,
but the Lord has the final authority and say so.
Death has not written my biography!
The Lord my God knows my life from the beginning
to the end.

Though death may wander this wicked world for my
soul, I know that the Greater One dwells within me.
My inner man is as ferocious as a lion.
When one lives through the inner man, death,
pestilence, or Satan cannot withstand the power of God.

The Master can eradicate a nation within the blink of
an eye.
So why can't the Father destroy a pint-sized demon?

Living by faith and obeying the Father is how one must
get through in these last days.
More demons will begin to attack people like never before.
Satan is watching us, ready to pounce on us as if we were
doves in distress.

Demons are lurking and hiding around corners.
They are ready to destroy God's children.
The church has to be a powerhouse in these last days.
The church has to be ready to fight Satan head-on.

God's people have been petrified to stand up to Satan.
Satan uses fear to paralyze our faith.
Once you are paralyzed, you cannot defeat the Enemy.

The Enemy has been wearing a façade.
Many will be deceived by his so-called miracles.
But at the right time, the Lord will expose the Evil One.

Epic 44

Many people hold some form of religion.
Some people come in the name of Jesus, pretending
to be lovers of Christ Jesus.
These individuals are heading down the path of
destruction.

When someone is driven by demonic spirits,
they are enslaved to Satan.
Satan bombards a person's mind into thinking that
they can get away with wrongdoing.
The Enemy appears as your friend.

How can God and Baal be friends?
Light and darkness cannot be friends.
One cannot be on both ends of the spectrum.
You must decide whether to serve the kingdom of
God or the kingdom of darkness.

The Enemy blesses swiftly.
The Devil is a negotiator and will try to negotiate
one out of his salvation.
Satan will offer luxurious things and wealth but at a
price.

The Enemy chuckles in your face, but the minute you
are in trouble, he leaves you like a dying corpse.
Satan is a mass manipulator and the king of all lies.
Nothing is free in the kingdom of darkness.

One must sacrifice his soul if he wants wealth and
fame from Satan.
Wealth and fame are temporal,
but one's spirit and soul are eternal.

Jehovah-Jireh.promises His children wealth, and
God gives inheritances by grace.
When you enter the kingdom of God, your sins are
forgiven, and you are entitled to covenant privileges.
Our God is kind, winsome, gracious, and slow to anger.

When the Father blesses His saints, the blessings are
from His heart because He loves unconditionally.
When Satan blesses his family, he does it
because he wants their spirits.
The unjust judge flashes wealth like it is all his.

Satan wants the souls of many individuals.
In these last days, the Devil will come like a roaring
lion, leading many astray.
The Devil hides in the darkness of the night, awaiting
his next victim.

There are many lost in the world, O God.
Save the lost and dumbfounded from the hand of
the adversary.
Those who are growing weary, give them wings of
an eagle so they may soar to new heights.

O Father in heaven, save those who are prisoners
in Satan's camp.
Lucifer has a mighty stronghold on those who are
trying to escape him.
You are a God who sees, hears, and knows everything.
You are Adonai, the God who sees what is going on
behind the veil.

Remove the veil, O God, from those who desire to
see you.
Many people have been roaming the earth, seeking the
truth.
People are wandering from country to country, seeking
the chosen One.

Do not be misled into thinking that one must go to a
foreign land to get the truth.
The truth is that Christ is the chosen One.
Christ, the living God, exposed Himself to humiliation
so our spirits and souls would not be enslaved in
hell for eternity.

Be thankful, O saints of God, that through Jesus' death
we are able to stand in the Almighty's presence.
God is a just God.
The Lord is our vindicator, and whatever is wicked in
the sight of the Lord must go in Jesus' name!

There is power, might, and wisdom in Jesus' name.
God, who is the sovereign ruler of heaven and earth,
gave us a weapon for hostile situations.
The weapon is Jesus' name.

Every knee shall bow and every tongue shall
confess that Jesus is Lord! (Philippians 2:10-11)
Christians, come together and unite.
Harmonize together, saints of God, so we can abolish
the forces of darkness.

There is nothing too hard for God.
The Father designed us to have dominion over all
things.
We must go into Satan's kingdom and ravage his
territory.

Jehovah is raising leaders who do not fear death,
sickness, or Satan.
These radical leaders will eradicate territories that
are guarded by devils.
Those devils will flee because these fierce leaders
come in Jesus' name.

Demons know who you are.
The devils know who has a strong anointing to
cast out demons and pestilence.
Many are called but few are chosen. (Matthew 22:14)

Many people take the broad path in life.
Those who take the narrow more constricted
path endure more because of the call on their lives.
Obedience causes the Father to move on
one's behalf.

Though it may burn going through the fiery furnace,
know that with God all things are possible. (Matthew 19:26)
Pressure is put on us because God is molding us
into a masterpiece.
We must be pressed on both sides so our spirits
and souls are unblemished.
We may cry in agony and distress, but when Christ
has pulled us from the fire, we will be praising Him.

You will be like the Hope diamond, untainted and pure.
Because of what the Lord has done for me, no man,
beast, or devil can tear the bond I have with my Father.

My Father and I are one.
I will be with you until you are at rest with your forefathers.
Though your body is sleeping in the grave,
your spirit is alive and dancing with Me in paradise.

Epic 45

My heart yearns for people who do not reverse
the disastrous storms that are headed toward mankind.
Lord, have mercy on those countries that do not know.

The earth is filled with sin.
Do not allow tornadoes, hurricanes, tropical storms,
and raging fires to take the lives of the innocent.
Cover those nations and territories with the blood
of Jesus, O God.

Many will perish by the sword of Satan.
Famines, plagues, pestilence, and other forces of
darkness will consume the lives of many.
I am weeping in my spirit for those who are under
the curse of Satan.

There are wicked things taking place.
There are inhumane sacrifices occurring in the uttermost
parts of the world.
Ungodly countries are causing demonic storms to
ruin other countries and their people.
There are witches and warlocks who summon evil
spirits to take the lives of the innocent.

We must stay rooted and grounded in love.
Saints of God, hold fast to your confession of faith.
Satan will come from every angle to cause God's
children to give up.

God did not give up on us, so we as the Church must
not turn our backs on the Creator.
I was not created to be a stepping-stone for Satan.
I was created to ravage and annihilate Satan's kingdom.

Satan has caused pestilence to come upon the saints
of God.
The unjust judge has evoked illnesses that man cannot
diagnose.
These demonic sicknesses will try to consume the lives
of many.

I am a servant of the Master and Creator of heaven and earth.
I was struck with many illnesses.
From my infancy into adulthood, Satan has always had
a hit out on my life.
As a toddler, diseases would overtake my body.

My mother did everything in her power to get me
healed.
One day, Satan caused a demonic pestilence to wreak
havoc on my body.
Mother was dumbfounded and broken internally.

Though the doctor could not determine the diagnosis,
I knew I had to hold fast to my confession of faith.
I knew that Jesus the Healer would not forsake His
dying servant.

My spirit was dying because of the sicknesses injected
into my body.
My body is a temple of the living God.
Disease nor pestilence had a right to enter my body.

But the Lord my God breathed life, healing, and strength
into my mortal soul.
My soul wanted to give up and perish,
but Abba Father said, "Your time has not come for you
to be at rest."

My purpose is to serve God and bring the lost into the
kingdom of heaven.
My life is not my own; to You I belong.
When Christ died on the cross, I died with Him.

I must endure adversity as long as I am a servant of
the Lord.
The hell I have endured is not for my sake but rather
to reveal how Christ was with me and how He
delivered me.

You are my deliverer and redeemer, O God,
for had You not, O God, delivered me from the hand
of the Wicked One,
I would not be alive to tell my testimony.
Testimonies illustrate how one overcame the fiery
darts of the Wicked One.

The Wicked One has no power or sovereignty over me,
for the Lord has given me a weapon that shall make
Satan cry tears of blood,
for Satan has shed the blood of the innocent.

Avenge those who have died by the sword of the Wicked One.
Comfort those in mourning who have
lost loved ones by Satan.
You are my avenger, vindicator, and advocate, O God.

Those who harm Your servants shall be put to death,
dying a horrid and spiritual death.
God's people shall rejoice when the wicked are put to shame.

A dark cloud filled with shame and
hatred shall cover the wicked.
The wicked have no desire in fulfilling a godly life.
The wicked despise those who are close to the Lord.

The Lord will bring a great and mighty terror on the wicked.
The wicked will fall to their knees and
drown in their own evil ways.
A man's evil ways will never abort
him as long as he is enslaved
to the kingdom of darkness.

Evil days are near.
Times of turmoil and distress will try
to attack the body of Christ.
But we serve a God who is more powerful than any tornado.

Though tornadoes and hurricanes are trying one's spirit,
the Father has put a hedge of protection around us.
My ship may get tossed about on the raging seas,
but my Father has me anchored.

My spirit and soul are at peace.
I am like a ship navigating through
a swamp filled with devils.
The devils try to drown my ship in despair,
but the Lord is blowing a mighty wind in my direction,
a wind that will cause the devils to drown
in their pit of destruction.
Though destruction and torment may come, I know
that my words in the spirit realm are like
fire consuming anything evil.

When I open my mouth, fire will pour upon the ungodly.
The Father will breathe a devastating fire on the wicked.
I have a fire in me that eyes and ears have not seen or heard,
for the fire that God has placed in me is for eternity.
My fire shall never cease,
for I am on fire for the Lord.

When I go to be with my forefathers,
when I go to sleep in Abba Father's house,
my steps I have taken with God will be
felt by mankind worldwide.

Epic 46

Your holiness is beautiful, O Lord.
Fill me with Your magnificent presence for eternity,
for I will bless and cherish the Master in times of pain.

The pain I endure lasts momentarily,
for we are blessed with one life.
The Father blessed us with life so He can manifest
His glory through His people.

Jehovah-Jireh's presence is felt even in the darkest
places.
There is no escaping the Father.
The Father has His eyes set on everyone and everything.

Though the wicked chuckle in the darkness as God's
people endure adversity,
the Lord will raise them upon many nations,
for You are a God who shall not lie.
Your words are spirit and life.
Whatever His Majesty proclaims is ordained and
God-breathed.

The Father's words are precious and medicine to those
in dire distress.
Turmoil and shame may try to cover you,
but Abba Father has a pure heart filled with everlasting love.

One cannot earn the love of Christ.
You must receive Jehovah's love by faith.
Many have fallen by the hand of Satan, but the Lord
will avenge them of their adversary.

In the natural, Satan appears to be a
grotesque mighty warrior.
Lucifer is the father of all lies.
Satan is full of deception, anger, jealousy, hatred, and
other degrading things.

The unjust judge has evoked many injustices upon the
saints of God.
Satan does not fear man or beast.
Satan is a destroyer of mankind.
The Devil has put a veil over the eyes of mankind.

This wicked world is filled with sin and chaos.
This nebulous world is crying in distress.
Sin and wickedness have covered the face of the earth.

Satan is the ruler of this world.
The Devil has no clemency toward mankind.
The outside world has been brainwashed into believing
that God does not exist.

God so loved the world that he gave His
only begotten Son. (John 3:16)
Christ was sent to redeem us from the curse of the law.
The Father sent His precious Son so we would not suffer
a spiritual death.

Christ is the light of this world.
Satan despises the light and tries to keep the truth hidden.
God is the way, the truth, and the life. (John 14: 6)
He has come so we may have life more
abundantly. (John 10:10)

We are no longer enslaved to the kingdom of darkness.
The Almighty One has broken that power and cleansed us
from all unrighteousness.
Satan is not the author and finisher of our lives.

Our lives have been predestined by His Majesty.
His Majesty promises us peace, love,
joy, happiness, and longevity.
We shall eat the fruits of our labor and
dwell in a peaceful habitation.

Satan and his angels will come like a flood.
Satan will try to attack me with things like never before.
But the Father will fight my battles.
The battle is not mine; it is the Lord's.

We have an army on our side that is more robust than
any attack from Satan.
Satan, you have no power over me.
When I was baptized in Jesus' name, the water and
the blood of Jesus broke your authority.

As I went into the water, the Father
welcomed me with open arms.
As my spirit went into the water, a new spirit emerged.
A spirit of wisdom, boldness, excellency, honor, and might
covered my rejuvenated spirit.

I had to die so I could stand in the presence of the Lord.
Fallen angels wanted to stay attached to my soul,
so the Father consumed the old spirit with fire.

As I emerged from the waters, the real spirit came forth.
God's light broke forth as I became a new creature.
The manifestation of Christ and His
anointing engulfed my soul.

Christ is a gentlemen and a lover of those who worship Him.
In God is fullness and knowledge.
In Christ, we know we are well able
to conquer Satan's kingdom.

There is rest in Your tabernacle, O God.
When the storm comes, I will be like a tree firmly
planted by the still, calm waters.
Though the tide may try to drown me, my Father will
cause me to rise up on the raging waters.

Raging rivers will try to pull you back,
but do not fight the tide in your strength.
Use the anointing of God from within to destroy the storm.

Do not let the storm destroy you.
You become a destroyer!

Epic 47

I am in the lake of confusion,
for my flesh wants to abandon my God.
My God, O Lord of heaven and earth, why
dost thou allow me to be melancholy?

Though I walk in the day with a smile on my face,
in the darkness of the night, my soul weeps in distress.
How do you maintain your faith while in tribulation?
Tribulation, scarcity, anger, and resentment have
covered thy soul.

My soul aches in agony and anger.
When the sun shines through my bedroom,
my spirit is at peace.
The sun's rays from God's kingdom are like roses
blossoming on a summer's day.

Do not let the sun go down on your anger.
Satan laughs at the righteous when chaos and
confusion cover the souls of God's children.
We are swimming in a river whose current is
trying to detach us from the Father.

Do not quarrel with the current.
Let God's awesome Spirit within you propel
you down the river.
In the natural, it appears as if you are drowning,
but the Lord God has you in the palm of His hand.

Uncertainty, doubt, and anger have clouded my thoughts,
for doubt and uncertainty have crept into my soul.
My soul and spirit are at war.

There is a titanic struggle between aborting faith
and finding the will to go on.
God has injected me with a spirit of perseverance
and tenacity.
My flesh may be frail, but my spirit is robust like
my Father's.

The Almighty One fears no man, beast, or devils.
Satan is no match for the Father.
Lucifer is a fallen angel who is a counterfeit of Christ.
Christ knows the hidden deceptions that are planned
for God's people.
God's people are in a battle like no other.

Saints of God, get prepared because Satan is going to
launch an attack like never before.
Dig your heals deep in the Word of God.
Engulf yourself in your Father's presence.

Draw wisdom from Jehovah to destroy Satan and
his army.
There is infinite wisdom and knowledge in the Father.
Keep knocking and the door will be open unto you.

God pours water on thirsting ground.
Have a hungry and yearning spirit for Jehovah's
wisdom and revelation.
Remove the veil from our eyes, O God, so we may
see the hidden traps.

There are many pitfalls set to ensnare me.
Pitfalls that have been planned before I was formed
in my mother's womb.
But my Father has a pitfall for those who attack
God's children.

The Master's wrath is so ferocious that demons crawl
back into their beds of shame.
Though Satan may be the king of the underworld,
the Lord is the King of Kings and Lord of Lords.

His Majesty is the supreme ruler over every angelic spirit.
The Father has commanded His angels to encamp around us.
There are more for us than against us.

In the natural, it appears that Satan has outnumbered us.
But we serve a God who always fights our battles.

Our battles have been won prior to mankind being formed.
Before we were born, Lucifer saw the might and
valor that was bestowed upon us.
We are children of the Most High God.

We do not serve a God who is feeble.
We serve a God whose power no foe can withstand.
The power within the Father rests upon those who fear Him.

You are a great God and greatly to be praised.
We sing hymns, praises, and songs in
reverence of His Majesty.
His Majesty's throne is everlasting.

When one kingdom is destroyed, the Father will establish
a new kingdom.
As long as the earth rotates around the sun, and the
stars and moon glisten from the sea,
there will always be kingdoms falling by the sword
of other kingdoms.
But we serve a kingdom that supersedes any monarchy.

Men will lust after their own desires and ignore the
will of the Father.
Kings will be destroyed by gluttony and the lusts of
life,
but the Lord's throne will be on high.

Epic 48

O Father, God of Abraham, Isaac, and Jacob,
make my path straight, O God,
for it seems as though there is opposition.
This opposition has a grip on my soul and mind.

My mind and body want to stray from the Father,
but the inner man says to keep fighting the good
fight of faith.
My soul feels like it is weakening.

I am in a tug-of-war.
The battle between good and evil is always present.
Almighty God, send Your Son to heal my wounds
and transgressions.

I cannot do battle in human strength.
I must draw strength from my Father.
Abba Father's strength will quicken my weakened faith.

El Shaddai, help me stay rooted in Your Word.
Your Word, O God, is healing and medicine to my spirit.
My spirit yearns to be at one with the Father.

There is no other God but You.
When all else fails, the Word of God stands alone.
Breathe Your might into my spirit, O God.
O Father in heaven, calm the raging seas so
my soul will remain afloat.

Send forth a sign of Your goodness.
Sprinkle manna and the smell of sweet perfume
from the heavens.
You have not forgotten Your people, O God.

Wrap me in Your majestic arms, my King.
You are a king who is greatly to be praised.
I will worship You in spirit and in truth.

Your holiness is beautiful, O Lord.
Though I cannot see You and have nothing tangible,
I know that my redeemer lives.
You, O God, are forever with Your servant.
I will not leave you nor forsake you.

Fiery darts and attacks are headed toward me,
but I will be bold as a lion.
I am from the tribe of Judah.

I am my Father's daughter.
I am not afraid of anything.
I was born into a kingdom whose power no foe
can withstand
and whose king has an army with an infinite number
of soldiers.

We are in a war, O servants of the living God.
Satan is launching attacks against the just.
The Tempter has caused disastrous winds and
demonic storms to overtake the righteous.

Many evil have confronted the just.
These evil spirits have crept their way into the
lives of God's people.
These demonic spirits cause strife, rebellion, and anger.

But Jehovah will cause a fatal pestilence and
punishment to come upon the wicked.
Even though there are people against me, there
are more for me.
We do not wrestle against flesh and blood, but
against principalities, the rulers of this dark world,
and spiritual wickedness in high places. (Ephesians 6:12)

Though I cannot see the Father, I know He is on my side.
If God can be for me, who can be against me? (Romans 8:31)
Many evils confront the righteous,
but the Lord shall deliver him out of them all. (Psalms 34:19)

You have Your children in the palm of Your hand.
His Majesty will not be made a mockery of.
His Majesty will be on the throne for all eternity.
Even though storms, earthquakes, tornadoes, and
other disasters will occur,
His Majesty is still on the throne.
Though we may be in this nebulous world filled with evil,
there is a kingdom that will never be annihilated,
and that is the kingdom of heaven.

Send forth Your glory, Jehovah.
Send forth Your warrior angels to
encamp around Your people.
People are being led astray, O God,
grab them with a mighty hand.

Fill me with Your presence, Father, so I may be
able to stand in the evil days.
Cover my spirit and soul with Your strength and might.
Strength, might, and valor are in the Spirit of God.

Draw wisdom and inspiration from the Father's belly.
The Father's belly is filled with wisdom and knowledge
that supersedes all science.

The natural man rationalizes science as the answer
to mankind's dilemmas.
But the godly man draws wisdom from the Father
because He reveals His mysteries unto His servants.

God has hidden treasuries for the godly.
Wisdom is a treasure.
He who has wisdom is rich in mind, body, soul, and spirit.

The Spirit searches the heart.
The Spirit searches all things.
Out of the abundance of the heart, the mouth speaks.

Lord, help me to speak good things,
for by my words, I shall be justified or condemned.
When I stand before the Father, I want Him to say,
"Job well done. Your journey is complete.
Now you may rest, my daughter."

Epic 49

God, I am torn between spirit and flesh.
God of Abraham, Isaac, and Jacob,
give Your servant strength to withstand the evil days.
My spirit desires to please the Father, but the
flesh wants to give into temptation.

The Tempter utilizes spirits to tempt God's
children into doing lustful and sinful things.
The spirits of lust, fornication, and homosexuality
hover over these sinful streets.
Lust and fornication haunt the streets for my
immortal spirit.

The smell of lust and fornication have tried to
attach itself to my domain.
Abba Father, keep me rooted and grounded in love.
Father God, help me to see when I am in danger.

O Master in heaven, protect Your servant from the
Wicked One.
The Wicked One wants my innocence and purity.
Satan wants me to go down a path of destruction
and turmoil.
Satan has hidden snares set for God's people.

Satan is the ruler of deception and wants God's
children to be in the pit of hell.
Deception has covered the earth for thousands of years,
but the Lord my God has sent His Spirit to protect
the righteous.

I have not seen the righteous forsaken.
The Father sent His only begotten Son that
we could be made the righteousness in Christ Jesus.
Jesus redeemed us from the curse so we
could have sonship with Him.

Saints of God, desire to be at one with the Father.
My spirit yearns to be at rest with my Father.
The Spirit searches all things and the
uttermost parts of our being.

The Spirit searches the hearts and minds of men.
The Holy Spirit was sent to dwell within us.
The Holy Spirit is our teacher, leader,
instructor, and advocate.

How could we lose if the Holy Spirit is our teacher?
The Holy Spirit was placed in this demonic world
so He may guide us through the murky swamps.
There are many roads available, but the road less
traveled leads to pain and conflict for bearing the
name of Christ.

The wider the road, the more people.
The narrow road has more pressure.
Pressure and heat are Satan's weapons in defeating
the saints.

Though the pressure and heat become difficult to bear,
the Holy Spirit causes our spirits to rise
and fight the good fight of faith.

We were not promised an easy life,
but God came bear our burdens and yokes.
Yokes are hard to carry,
but the Lord has destroyed the yokes and burdens
through the anointing.

The anointing is a powerful weapon that causes
demons to crawl back into the underworld.
I am drowning in sorrow and heartache.
My soul weeps, for my heart and faith is weakening.

Satan is attacking my spirit and soul like never before.
I am surrounded by barriers and fortresses.
Abba Father, remove the forces of darkness.

The unjust judge has plagued me with many fiery darts.
These darts have pierced my soul,
for I am being crushed with a mighty blow.

Resurrect my decaying soul.
Breathe strength, might, and valor into Your servant, O God.
I am growing weary in the battle;
angels of the Lord, I command thee to eradicate the wicked.

Jehovah, reach forth from Your throne
and save Your servant.
Ride Your chariots of fire surrounded by warriors, O Lord,
and comfort me.

Open up the windows of heaven.
Pour out upon me a blessing where there shall not be
room enough to receive it.
Show me a sign of Your favor, O God.
A sign to Satan that You have not forgotten to
reward Your faithful servant.

Though melancholy and anger try to cover my soul,
I will still bless the Lord at all times,
for He is the author and finisher of my life.

Epic 50

Saturate this place with Your presence, Father.
Shower Your children, O God, with favor,
loving-kindness, and tender mercies.
Comfort Your saints, O God.

Remove the cloud of shame and guilt from Your
servants.
The nebulous clouds and storms have encamped
around me.
Raging waters and demonic storms have tried to
drown me.

Though I was born into warfare, the Father has
blessed me with a ferocious weapon,
the sword, which is the Word of God.
I am running the race my Father has called me to.

I am on a journey that will leave a legacy.
His Majesty called me to perform
wondrous signs and miracles,
but I must fight so people will see
that I am a walking wonder.

I will not turn away from my Father in heaven.
Heaven is cheering me on to victory.
Victory, honor, courage, and valor were injected into
my new spirit.
My Father and I are inseparable; a unity that no devil,
Human, or beast can destroy.

Cover those in shame, Jehovah, who despise and detest
Your statutes.
Shut the mouths of those who speak
evil against the living God.
Those who want Your servant to fall, O Lord,
dig a pit of destruction for them.

Wickedness, filth, and uncleanness are
upon the face of the earth.
Resurrect those who are broken in spirit.
Jesus, raise those radicals so they may see that You are alive.

Release favor upon Your servant.
Consume those with fire who make a mockery of You.
You are a just God.
Those who do evil will perish by the sword.

Slice the tongues of the wicked.
Those who do evil in the darkness,
exploit their unclean ways.
Shut the mouths of the false prophets,
preachers, and teachers.

Those who lead God's people astray shall be no more.
Wipe out the evildoers from the kingdom of God.
Drive out the demons who are running the pulpits.

Cover the wicked with a cloud of shame and torment.
Reverse the curse, O God, that has
been sent to Your children.
Exploit the demons who wreak havoc.

Show the world and dark places Your power is alive and
ready to be displayed.
Expose those who make a mockery of the faithful.
The righteous shall never be put to shame.

Consume the evildoers with a pestilence.
Break the jaws and teeth of those who speak treachery.
Dismantle the arms and legs of those who wreak havoc.

Father, clothe those who hide in darkness with torture.
Go to the uttermost parts of the earth,
O God, and expose the Devil.
Beat the pillars, and eradicate the
underworld with Your wrath.

Those who worship idols shall burn in the lake of fire.
All of the soothsayers, sorcerers, and witches shall be
tormented for eternity.
Curse those who curse Your servant, Lord.

You are the Lord of Lords and King of Kings.
There is no other God besides You.
You are a gracious God and slow to anger.

Convict the sinner, O God, in his heart.
Draw nigh to those who are lost, Addonai.
Shower the earth with Your glorious works.

You will be forever praised.
Fill the earth with the fullness of Your love, knowledge,
and revelation.
Rain manna from the heavens, O God.

Place Your servant over many nations.
Anoint Your servant and crown me with loving-kindness
and tender mercy.
Saturate my mind, body, soul, and spirit
with Your presence, Father.

Release favor, deliverance, and the goodness of the Lord.
Call forth those, O God, to spread the gospel.
Manifest Yourself, O God, so Your presence
will leave a legacy, even after Your return.

Epic 51

My soul and spirit are in distress.
I cry, "Abba Father, Jehovah-Jireh, have mercy on me.
I have grown weary from the turmoil in my life."

I am in the dark, and my footsteps know not the
direction to go.
I am in a spiritual battle.
The Lord and Satan both want my spirit.

My back is against the wall.
I am walking through the darkness of the night,
trying to unlock doors.
Doors that do not unlock and indecisiveness covers me.

Break forth Your bright light in this murky situation, O God,
for I am lost in an unknown world
and a circumstance over which I have no control.

I humbly ask my King, "Why do You put Your humble
servant in the fiery furnace?"
The fiery darts are burning the flesh of Your servant.
I am being molded into the image of my Father in heaven.
The crushing, brokenness, and heartaches are
part of being a disciple of Christ.

Remove thy servant from the furnace, Jehovah.
Remove the heat of affliction from my mind, body, and soul.
I am at a loss for words, for the darkness has consumed me.

I will soon reach the shore and my God-given destiny.
My destiny is not to remain in the place of sheol
but to triumph over Satan and his army.

Satan's army is strategic and methodical.
Satan studies details and how God's people react in adversity.
Satan will utilize any type of warfare
to detach us from the Father.
Satan uses situations, people, curses,
vexations, and demons to hinder our walk with God.
The Creator's Spirit is forever with His people.
The Father is on the throne, breathing
rejuvenation into our spirits.

His Highness is aware of the obstacles we must endure.
Nevertheless, we must run the race
that God has set before us.
I must bear my own cross.

The cross I bear is heavy and tenacious.
Before I was formed in my mother's womb,
God injected me with a spirit to never give up.
In the face of adversity, in the face of Satan and his
devils, I will not give up!

I will be bold toward Satan, demons, sickness, and hell.
I will not hide in the sea for fear of Satan.
I am a warrior in God's army and am not afraid of anything.

I am a soldier for the King of Kings.
Long live the King! For it is He who has injected might,
valor, and tenacity into my spirit.
Though other kingdoms may perish,
the kingdom of God will forever reign,
even after the earth is eradicated.

Even though the kingdom of God is an invisible empire,
the Lord is still ruler over all.
There is a titanic war taking place in the natural.
It appears that Satan is winning, but the
Almighty One knows and sees the beginning from the end.

Pestilence and natural disasters shall sweep across the land,
but it shall not come nigh God's people.
The Lord has put a hedge of protection
around those who fear Him.
We serve a God of clemency who is
filled with unconditional love.

Love, peace, joy, clemency, wisdom, and
reverential fear of the Lord
are in the Father's belly.
The love, peace, happiness, joy, power, and sound mind
have been injected into our spirits.
The Father loves His children and shall protect us and
hide us under His wing.
The Father's wings are so massive and heavy
that no fiery dart can penetrate it.
Abba Father is a rescuer and strong tower to the hopeless.
God's chariots of fire are filled with power.

Weapons may be aimed at God's chariots,
but the Lord's wrath will consume those who are against
His children.
No weapon formed against me shall prosper. (Isaiah 54: 17)
Any tongue that rises against me in condemnation
shall be put to shame.
Weapons will form, but the Lord will consume those
who do evil.

Satan is coming to mimic the Creator.
The unjust judge will seat himself on high
and declare that he is god.
But the Lord will unveil and expose the Antichrist.

The Antichrist shall perish by the sword of the Almighty
One.
Those who follow the Antichrist shall be clothed in
torture and torment.
The lake of fire shall consume the wicked.

Screams of torture and torment shall cover the evildoers.
They will beg for clemency, but the Lord will
turn His back while evoking a sentence of eternal death.

Those who wait on the Lord shall renew their strength
like eagles and mount close to God. (Isaiah 40:31)
Those who follow Christ shall have everlasting peace
and take comfort in His Majesty's bosom.

Epic 52

Why do You allow me to suffer?
My soul is yearning for dire help from the Father.
Why do You allow adversity to overtake Your servant?

We are in perilous times,
for the kingdom of almighty God is at
war with Satan's kingdom.
Satan is growing more robust than ever before.

My spirit and soul are in deep distress,
for I am a spirit wandering through a
demonic and chaotic world.
I am lost in the darkness,
and the nebulous clouds hover over my being.

My spirit, soul, and body are growing
faint due to fiery trials of life.
My soul and body says, "The Lord has disowned His servant
and takes pleasure in observing His daughter suffer."

My soul wants to cave in and go into the world.
My soul and spirit are in a titanic
struggle between good and evil.
Though I reside in a world where things are temporal,
the Lord has yet to pull me from the place of the dead.

I have asked Jehovah, "How long shall You persecute me?
How long shall I suffer the whip lashes of Satan?"
I am like the walking dead, whose
spirit is wallowing in agony.

Your servant is on the verge of a spiritual death, my Lord.
Though the God of Abraham, Isaac, and Jacob slays me,
my spirit shall serve the living God.

The Creator of heaven and earth holds the keys to eternal
life and eternal torment.
The almighty God is a just God but is not fair.
The Father has everyone in the palm of His hand.
My life was predestined before the Holy of Holies formed me
in my mother's womb.
Though I may be in the fiery furnace,
Satan will not annihilate me.

Satan is not the author and finisher of my life.
Christ is the head of my life and ruler of my destiny.
Destiny was birthed into my spirit when
God called me as His daughter.

When a true servant of the Lord walks upright,
all the forces of darkness will attack.
Though your destiny may be within your reach,
sometimes your calling is birthed in tumultuous times.

Though we may not hear the Father's majestic voice,
we must believe that He is guiding our footsteps.
Wherever the souls of your feet tread,
that have I given you. (Joshua 1:3)
Our footsteps are our identity with the Father.

Though tears of agony may stream down my face,
the pain in my soul is temporary.
My spirit shall continue to fight until I meet my Creator.

Epic 53

The unjust judge is trying to alter the plans
the living God has for His daughter.
Though this wicked world is trying to pull my
soul into the underworld,
my soul will fight the good fight of faith.
Though I may be crying tears of melancholy,
the Lord my God is wiping them away.

Every tear that I have shed,
the Creator has kept in a bottle.
There is no sadness, sickness, or death in heaven,
for in heaven, the spirit and soul are at rest with the Father.

The Father wraps His majestic arms around those who
are in distress.
Adonai's heart is filled with love for His children.
Though my soul may not comprehend
the adversity I am enduring,
my spirit is at peace with the King of Kings.

Jesus is Lord and ruler over heaven and earth.
Jesus holds the keys to heaven and hell.
Choose life, for when you do, you shall
eat the fruit of the land.

Devoting one's life to the Messiah is a
precious gift that Satan despises.
Satan is an illusionist who perverts the work of the Lord.
The Lord knows the thoughts of mankind
and searches the hearts of men.

Mankind is lost in the wilderness.
Man believes that he is god and can do without God.
Mankind's intelligence is inferior to the
wisdom in the Father's belly.

Wisdom flows from the Lord's belly into His servant's spirit.
My spirit yearns for godly wisdom and the knowledge
of His resurrection.
There is power in His resurrection.

When Christ was resurrected, He
brought us into the presence
of the almighty God.
When one is resurrected, it brings forth a new spirit
in the living God.
The resurrection terminated Satan's reign on earth.

Satan is locked in the pit of hell for eternity.
Lucifer's strength and power is feeble compared
to the might and valor that is in Yahweh.
Yahweh will for eternity be the true judge and living God.

No other gods shall supersede Jehovah.
God has spoken things, and the power from His lips caused
things to exist.
If God had not spoken me into existence,
I would have been a nonentity.

The Lord spoke my spirit and soul into existence
because there is an assignment I must complete.
Though Satan is quarreling with me, my journey shall
be fulfilled because of God's mighty power within me.

Epic 54

Why do You put Your servant in
situations I do not want to be in?
The unjust judge chuckles in the darkness at my downfall.
Satan desires my life because I am a
severe threat to the underworld.

The underworld desires for my soul
and spirit to be in torment.
Satan wants me to turn my back on the living God.
Though God allows me to stay in tumultuous times,
my spirit will forevermore serve the Master.

Though God allows me to be attacked by Satan,
I know Jehovah is preparing me for what lies ahead.
The road I am walking with the Father is filled with danger.

When one decides to devote his or her life to God,
Satan will unleash his demons.
Lucifer despises Jesus, for he knows that God's army,
along with His servants, will terminate
Satan and his kingdom.

We are in a world filled with chaos and demons
These demons have come to reign and recruit people
into the kingdom of darkness

The kingdom of darkness is filled with lies, false hope,
murder, and worship of false gods.
I am in a battle between good and evil.
Both Jehovah and Satan long for my spirit.

Though Satan may attempt to proposition me,
the Lord is still guiding my footsteps into the life He
has ordained for me.
Even though the Father is silent at times,
I know He has me in the palm of His hand.
My strong tower, protector, and avenger will never
forsake His servant.

Once you give your life to almighty God, you become a
a warrior in God's army.
God's army is invisible and detrimental to Satan's army.
Even though Satan believes he is the master ruler,
Christ is going to return and demolish him.

There will come a time when the unjust judge and
his devils will become nonexistent.
The Lord will forever reign when Armageddon is complete.
But I tell you, good citizens of Christ, fear not,
for the God we serve is more robust than any spirit!

There are many spirits wandering this realm.
There are many voices that try to imitate the Holy Father.
But Your spirit knows when it is the King of Glory
because He comes with peace and truth.

Even though I may be a woman in the flesh,
I choose to have the heart of my Father.
My spirit is so dynamic and filled with might that
Satan trembles at my footsteps.
My footsteps will be embedded on the hearts and
souls of mankind.

Even though I was born into combat, my words,
which are a sword, will defeat and
burn Satan to his rotten core.

Epic 55

There is a sense of peace that shelters my spirit and soul.
As I sit on the sands that Jehovah has created,
I sense the Almighty's presence.
As my eyes look out onto the powder blue ocean,
my soul is at peace.

Serenity, peace, and tranquility is where my soul lies.
Master of heaven and earth, pour out Your grace
and love upon Your servant.

My soul and spirit are at rest with the Father.
Abba Father, wrap Your servant in Your majestic arms.
I yearn to be at peace with the King of Kings.

My heart is filled with happiness and joy despite
the tumultuous times I have endured.
Though I may be young in the flesh,
I have the heart and soul of a wise man.

I long for Abba Father to shower me with His
infinite wisdom and revelation.
O Lord, draw me into our secret place of worship.
Though sometimes I feel solo in a world of evil,
I know the Greater One dwells within me.

Show me a sign of Your favor, O God.
Send forth a blessing that eyes and
ears have not seen or heard.
Punish those who curse You and bless those who
have a heart pure toward Christ.

Search the hearts of mankind, O God.
Uproot and pluck all of the evildoers who are
against the Sovereign Lord.
Those who fear the Lord shall have a peace that passeth
all understanding.

I may not understand why the Father does the things
He does.
Mankind can rationalize in their minds about God.
Nevertheless, we serve a God whose intelligence
and wisdom supersedes any genius.

My heart desires to have the mind and body of Christ.
Bless me, O God, with such wisdom that mankind
will wonder what manner of woman is this.
Seek the Lord with all your heart and soul,
and He will guide your path and footsteps.

Listen to the Father.
Your spirit knows when Christ is speaking.
There is a peace beyond what mankind can comprehend.

God is sending me in a direction where people will
be amazed at my abilities.
I will soar to new heights with the Father.
The Father is guiding my spirit into the destiny
He has predestined for His servant.

I am on a journey and am not looking back.
I am soaring through the skies and living out the
dream the Lord has instilled within me.
I will fly like an eagle, and my spirit shall remain calm
regardless of the storms.

Epic 56

As I roam this world, I wonder, has the Lord
my God forgiven me?
I have done things that were not pleasing
in the Father's sight.
I am torn between two worlds.

The Father is calling me to be at peace
and have an intimate relationship with Him.
Satan wants me to serve him so he can abuse my gift.

Though I question many things that the almighty God
allows in my life, there is a purpose for them
Gifting and anointing causes much heartache.
Whatever treasures are buried in my soul,
I pray that Jehovah will release them.

I am being molded into the woman the Lord has
called me to be.
The process I am enduring is beyond painful.
Sweat, tears, and melancholy have hovered over my being
these past years.

I ask the King, "When are You going to release Your
servant from the fiery furnace?
How long must this season last before I receive the
crown of glory?"

My mind tries to comprehend the thoughts of the Father.
Though I will never be able to figure out the mind of God,
I know He has the final say in my ending.

Endings are far more superb than beginnings
because one will look at the tumultuous journey
that had to be endured.
I am on a journey that is far beyond my control.
Deep within my core, I must believe that Abba
Father is guiding me into my God-given destiny.

There will be roadblocks, obstacles, and other
detours along my path.
There will be mountains that will try to crush what
God has ordained me to do.
Even though obstacles will attempt to crush my soul,
the weapons of Satan shall not crush my spirit.

Satan sees something within me that I am trying to discover.
Satan is the king of lies and author of perversion.
Though Satan sees my gifts, he will
not be able confiscate them
because of the divine protection around my soul.

There are more imposters trying to solicit people
into the kingdom of darkness.
These imposters speak with eloquence and knowledge
about God that makes them appear
as true worshippers of God.
But underneath the decorative
ornaments lies a ravenous beast.

These people are manipulative and
blinded by their own evil ways.
I tell you, be mindful how you use the Scriptures,
for if they are utilized incorrectly, one's
spirit is damned for eternity.

Woe to you who leads innocent people astray,
for your time shall come when the beasts and demons
from hell shall feed upon your flesh.
There is a struggle between God and Satan.
Satan has established territories that are
ruled by demonic influences.

Many so-called teachers will appear from other lands,
but the Father will expose their lies and secrets.
I tell you, good citizens of God, do not be petrified
when the Tempter tests your faith.

There will come a time when we must
decide which master to serve.
We cannot serve both God and mammon.
We will love one and hate the other.

You cannot be friends with Satan and
expect the Lord to bless you.
God is a just God and blesses whoever He wants.
Gird the faith that God has instilled into your spirit
so in times of distress, you can beat
the Devil at his own game.

False prophets, teachers, and leaders roam
the streets, seeking the weak.
But the Master has His eyes on everybody.
Nobody can escape the day of judgment.

In these last days, the King of Glory is breeding
His soldiers and leaders to eradicate Satan.
Even though these demons believe they have dominion,
the Creator is going to breathe a catastrophic
storm that no beast can withstand.

Those who try to escape the presence of the Lord
shall be caught and dehumanized before the people of God.

These demons sent by Satan are going
to be burned in their spirits.
God is the Creator of heaven and earth.
He is also the Creator of hell.
If you do evil, your bed shall be made in hell,
and God's Spirit will still be there.

Epic 57

As I lie on the bed of pain, I wonder,
will I go to heaven?
As I lie on pins and needles, I often ask, "Will
the Father welcome me with open arms?"
You are a just God and faithful to cleanse me
of my sins, O Lord.

I know I have indulged in things that are not of You, my Lord.
I have afflicted myself for many decades.
As I lie in turmoil and distress,
the darkness and the light battle for my soul and spirit.

When I look in the mirror of melancholy,
I see hurt and feel distraught.
I have allowed Satan to poison my
soul with deadly substances.
When my kindred abandoned me,
illicit substances were my comforter.

As a little boy, my parents did not demonstrate
true love and affection.
My earthly parents' only care was financial stability.
Money was my parents' priority.

I come from a family that lacked unconditional love.
Since an adolescent, I have had the spirits of
inferiority, obsession, and addiction hover over my being.
These demonic spirits have a hold upon my being.

I am lost in the darkness and am a
prisoner of the underworld.
Satan has had my soul and spirit in
bondage since I was a young man.
The spirits of torture, suicide, and
insanity have surrounded me
like vultures feeding on a rotten corpse.

The unjust judge is planning my demise
along with his many legions.
I am weak, O King, for the forces of
darkness are mightier than me.
I am drowning in the pool of suicide.

The spirit of death engulfs me like bees sticking to honey.
I am trapped in a place where light does not exist.
Only the wickedness of the night prevails
in a world filled with chaos.

My spirit and soul can no longer see the light.
My eyes and spirit grow weary from
the abuse of the Wicked One.
Satan gets glory out of dehumanizing my soul.

I am no match for the unjust judge.
My body grows feeble as the days grow shorter.
My inner being is distraught and filled with pain.

I am roaming through the underworld.
I am wandering through the earth with no sense of who I am.
Satan has confiscated my identity.

Without my identity and integrity, I will forever
be enslaved by the Wicked One.
Remove a man's self-worth and dignity,
and he has no life.

Losing one's identity and spirit to Satan is
detrimental in the eyes of the Lord.

There is nothing too difficult for the Creator.
The Master can take a man who has been
abused spiritually and re-create him into the
God-fearing man He has called him to be.

Many are called but few are chosen. (Matthew 22:14)
The road to living a Christ-life requires one
to withstand the inflammable darts of the Wicked One.
But the road to redemption is but a step away.

Our Redeemer lives for eternity.
Long live our devoted King,
for He is the King of Kings and Lord of Lords.
He is the supreme ruler over all
and holds the keys to heaven and hell.

Epic 58

Why does Your heart keep being broken by man?
Lord, You said You would turn Heartbreak
Valley into Acres of Hope.
Even though many have hurt my heart,
the Lord my Savior is the only One who has my heart.

Heavenly Father, I do not know the path in
which You are leading thee.
But in all my ways, I shall acknowledge the Lord,
and He shall direct my paths. (Proverbs 3:6)

The Lord is close to those of a broken heart. (Psalms 34:18)
I shall not give my heart unto another man.
Mankind will fail you.

But we serve a God who holds our success in the
palms of His hands.
His hands hold the key to our destiny.
My faith shall create things the natural
man cannot comprehend.

The power and sovereignty the Master
has bestowed upon me
shall startle the underworld.

Thank You, Jehovah, for making me grow robust
in times of distress.
Even though I may be a woman in the flesh,
I have the soul and spirit of my Father.
My Father has a Spirit no man or beast can withstand.

Even in my darkest moments, the
Lord of Host is still with me.
My eyes have yet to see the King of Glory,
but the Father's presence shall last even
after the day of judgment.

As planets and galaxies rotate clockwise,
the Spirit of the Lord is everywhere.
As the cosmos, galaxies, and other elements of space collide
with one another,
the Lord of Hosts still stands for eternity.

The things that are seen are subject to change
at any given moment.
But the things that are not made in the flesh
but are manifested by the Spirit will last for eternity.

Whatever God has declared and ordained shall come to pass.
Whatever God has mandated and considered as law shall
never be subject to transformation.

The laws of the government metamorphose continuously.
But the laws of heaven shall reign and
not be judged by a democracy.
Even though we are good citizens of Christ,
we still have to obey the laws of government.
But we are obligated to remain true to
the government in heaven.

We are to obey Christ and never worship any idol gods!
At times, God will allow adversity to fall upon us,
but we shall never return unto Baal!

Baal is a manipulative god that uses deception
and illusion to brainwash others.
Even though Baal is the master of deception and lies,
the Father's eyes are still roaming through
the darkest parts of the world.

Light and darkness will always despise each other.
But when Abba Father's Spirit shines forth in dark places,
the darkness must go.

Light and darkness cannot dwell in one place,
for the light shall destroy the powers of darkness.
Even though we are in a nebulous world,
God's Spirit will ravage every wicked thing.

There are some things we are not able to see,
but the Lord of Host is in places bringing
down rulers of wickedness in high places.
The rulers of the night believe they are invisible,
but the Lord my God shall snatch them from
their high places and beat them small.

They shall be no more.
These wicked rulers will be forgotten and leave no legacy.
But the Lord will leave His powerful
footprint upon their souls.

Epic 59

I have found my true love, and it is the
Creator.
The King and I are bonded together for eternity.
O King, I know the best is yet to come.

You are my King, and I am Your queen.
My Lord, You adore me and show me
true, unconditional love.
The love of my Husband supersedes all erotic desires.

When I cried out to You, my Lord,
You saved me and wiped away the tears from my face.
Every tear that has streamed down my face
You have kept in a bottle.
My Husband, You are a man of great valor and integrity.

My Lord, You and I are united in s spiritual
marriage before the foundation of this world.
You and I are one, Jehovah.
Wherever I go, O God, You are there with me for eternity.

Cherish me, dear Husband,
Your soul, love, and honor commit unto me.

My Lord, You have prepared a unity for us that
no devil or beast can rip apart.
Though Satan will try to tempt my marriage with
lust, lies, and deceit,
the Father will bless it with magnificent strength.
Lord, You are a man who shalt not lie.

Together we shall soar like birds entering
into another dimension.
My Lord, You and I shall demolish Satan's kingdom.
The Father has blessed us and given us the grace
to defeat the enemies of darkness.

Marriage is a gift from the Father.
When a man and woman are joined together for eternity,
they take a vow unto the Lord.
Lord bless this marriage that You have
ordained before the heavens.

God rejoices when He unites a man and woman spiritually.
The Lord has called me to be a virtuous and devoted wife.

God is the head of Christ,
Christ is the head of the church,
and man is the head of the woman.
Even though my husband is my head,
Jehovah called me to be His help me mate before
He formed us in our mothers' wombs.

You and I will leave our marks on earth.
Our footsteps shall be imprinted on the hearts of men.
Your words shall be embedded upon many nations.

You and I are one in spirit.
We shall be led by the Spirit and defeat many nations.
Our children shall carry on the legacy
we have imparted to them.
When we die and our bodies are lying in the grave,
our spirits shall meet in heaven,
but our presence shall be felt by mankind.

Epic 60

Let the redeemed of the Lord have joy, peace,
and tranquility on earth.
Our Redeemer shall live for eternity,
for we shall give continuous praise unto our
Savior Jesus Christ.

Come into the Lord's presence with an open heart
and receive the wondrous gifts He has
bestowed upon His people.
Enter into His gates with thanksgiving and praise.
Enter into His Majesty's court with
honor, praise, and worship.

Worship the Lord in the beauty of His essence.
O God of Abraham, Isaac, and Jacob,
bestow your grace upon my soul and spirit.
Give Your servant a heart and mind that is pure toward You.

Prepare Your people, Jehovah, for the radical faith
that one must have to defeat the powers of darkness.
Darkness, demons, pestilence, and
spells have no place on earth.
God intended the earth to flourish like the heavens.

Though we may be at war with the forces of darkness,
our Master shall bring these fallen angels to their knees.
Even though there are opposing forces,
we as good citizens of the Lord have a mighty army
that shall fight our battles.
The battle is not mine; it is the Lord's.

The Lord of Hosts is filled with honor, valor, and might.
The Master fears nothing and no one.
The Great One has such dynamic strength
that even sea creatures bow at His feet.

We serve a King who is far more superior and robust
than any earthly king.
God has kingdoms set upon this earth.
But in this time and realm, we serve a
kingdom that shall last for eternity.

God, who is the only true God, is the
sovereign ruler of this world.
You shall not put any gods before Me. (Exodus 20:3)
There is no power in worshipping idol gods.
The true power is in worshipping the Creator of the heavens.

The righteous shall inherit the earth.
You shall be planted among the wicked,
but the Lord's Spirit that engulfs your inner man
shall cancel the darkness.

Earth is like a deep, nebulous hole.
The earth is weeping tears of melancholy, hurt, and distress.
This place is filled with such hatred that the
earth can no longer bear the burden.

Jesus is weeping for the people,
for they hold a form of respect for the Great One.
They hold a form of religion but have no love for Christ.

Christ wants us to shine forth His Spirit upon the needy.
Show mercy to those who know not the ways of the Lord.
Show mercy and love to others
and it shall be reciprocated to thee.

The church is supposed to be a place of true honor
and unconditional love for the people and for worship.
God is to represent the church.
Man is God's vessel to deliver ordained
messages from heaven.

Mankind wants the glory because of his so-
called knowledge and intellect.
Intellect can get you just so far;
one must have the infinite wisdom of
the Father to do the impossible.

There are no limits with the Master.
We allow Satan to create boundaries
and limitations in our lives.
God is a Spirit who calls forth things into existence.

Allow the Father to use you.
Speak only what His Majesty says.
Whatever the King says is law and must be ordained.
We are kings and queens of the Most High God.

Though you are planted among the wicked,
do not allow evil to overtake you,
but overtake evil with good.
As long as the earth rotates clockwise, and the
planets are in alignment with each other,
the Lord still reigns.

Jehovah has the universe and the people in the
palm of His hand.
Though Satan throws fiery darts,
the Master will never release his
people from His mighty hand.

Epic 61

The Lord my God is more powerful than
any foe upon this earth.
Lord, save me from the hand of the Wicked One.
Avenge me of mine adversary.

As the world grows more nebulous and wicked,
I find myself entangled in things that are not of You.
Darkness, wickedness, and death surround my being.
I often weep about the things I have committed.

My past seems to be after me.
The things I have done and seen haunt
me in the midnight hour.
Save me, Jehovah, from my past.

Satan terrorizes my mind with wicked things of the past.
You know the thoughts and heart of man.
My heart is filled with sorrow and pain, O Lord.

The Lord who created me in my mother's womb,
the Master who has called things
naught as though they were,
the Lord who called me into existence.

Stir that Holy Spirit, O God.
Give me a heart, O God, that is pure
and sensitive to Your voice.
Restrain my flesh from temptation.

Cover me with Your majestic wings.
Extend Your loving-kindness and tenderness upon me.
for my soul and spirit are covered by darkness.

I am surrounded by demons and
creatures of the underworld.
Satan knows how to get one's attention.
The unjust judge studies people and tempts them
with what appears to be a blessing.

Lucifer is a master manipulator and liar.
Satan tempts me with riches, lust, and fame.
One must pay a price if he or she wants success and fame.
Fame is temporal, but one's soul is for eternity.

Give me rest and peace from the past, Abba Father.
Master, bless me with a calm spirit to withstand the tests
and fiery darts from hell.
Save my soul from eternal punishment.

Satan is plotting my demise.
The Devil has utilized those close to me to
wound my spirit and soul.
The Wicked One has his hook in my nose.

Lord, I pray that You will reveal to Your servant
who is of You and who is of the Devil.
The Devil will pervert things and send wicked
people to pull me toward the darkness.

My spirit and soul have dwelled in
darkness since I was a youth.
I have seen things that most people would dare not see.
My eyes have witnessed brutal and inhumane things.

When I was a little boy, I would gaze at the
stars and planets, hoping that the Lord would
transfer me to another dimension.
I saw images of horrific disasters to deter me
from my assignment.

Reveal unto me Your gifts and calling.
I have gifts in my spirit that are waiting to be released.

Crucify, destroy, and burn my soul and spirit.
Breathe new life and a new beginning into my soul.
Breathe, O God, spirit, might, wisdom, and valor upon me.
Remove Satan's grip from me.

Father, You have saved me from many catastrophes.
Satan has sent fatal storms to eradicate me.
Break the forces of darkness that have me in bondage.

Send forth a devastating storm to Satan and his army, O God.
Show the wicked that You really are my Lord.
A storm will engulf the wicked.
A storm will destroy the forces of darkness.

But You, O God, my redeemer and Father,
have covered me from Satan.
Though evil is seeking my life,
I have strength and might that no devil can withstand.

Bless those who bless me,
and curse those who curse me.
Shut the mouths and rip out the tongues of the soothsayers.

Even though spells, vexations, and curses are aimed at me,
the Lord of Hosts will reverse them and
send forth a deadly plague.
A plague so ferocious that mankind
will not have the intelligence
to figure it out.

Wrap me in Your arms, O God.
Cover me in Your bed.
Though I lie on a bed of melancholy,
turn my mourning into joy.

Redeem me from the hand of the wicked so
my spirit and soul are at rest in You, O God.

Epic 62

Lord, You are a wondrous and magnificent God.
I will bless You at all times, for it is You
who has blessed me more than I could imagine.
You are a great and awesome God.

No other gods shall reign before Jehovah.
No other gods have the power and
strength like the Almighty.
False gods and idols are blasphemous and disgusting in the
eyes of the Lord.

No other gods or demons can withstand
the Father's mighty blow.
When the Father releases His love and
blessings upon His people,
the unjust judge quivers in his spirit.
The more the Lord blesses His people,
the more damage they can do to Satan's kingdom.

The kingdom of darkness is filled with lies,
deception, false gods, and delusions of grandeur.
Once you enter into the kingdom of His Majesty,
you shall eat the fruit of the land and
be blessed in your spirit.

Bless those who bless Your holy name, O God,
and curse those who speak blasphemy and worship idol gods.
Pagan gods are worthless to the Lord.

The Lord despises pagan gods because it is He who created
the heavens and the earth.
Demons consider themselves gods
because they perform miracles.
But the miracles performed by the
creatures of the underworld
are doomed to eternal damnation.

How far will one go to achieve greatness?
Will you go to the dark side if God does not bless you?
Will you stick with Christ when it seems
like all the forces of darkness are opposing you?
Or will you allow Satan to deceive you with riches
in order to gain glory on earth?

Everyone wants success,
but some are willing to sell their soul and spirit to Satan.
Satan desires the souls of the lost because
he wants to be their ruler.

Even though Satan may think that he is the ruler over all,
the Lord is the King of Kings and Lord of Lords.
The Lord decides what takes place on earth.
The Father has ordained certain events and miracles
to take place before Satan was created.

Bless Your servants and warriors, O God,
with a spirit to withstand the fires from hell.
Bless Your children with strength, might, and valor
that no demon can withstand.
Terrorize the wicked who roam the earth,
trying to devour God's people.

Cast a deadly pestilence on those who
speak evil words against You.
The time shall come when we will rise as
mighty warriors and ravage the kingdom of darkness.

We are soldiers preparing for war.
We are a group of elite, God-fearing men and women.
We are part of an army that is more deadly than any force.

Raise the swords and defeat Satan.
Master, breathe fire upon the godless nations
so they may know You are the sovereign ruler.

Bring Your giants and warriors, O God,
to desolate and dark places.
Hunt the evildoers and expose their souls
and spirits to shame.
Burn those who create havoc for the innocent.

I am like a lion hiding in the bushes.
I will leap forth when God calls me
and rip those evildoers to pieces.
The evildoers shall be no more,
for the Lord of Hosts shall scatter them to and fro
over the earth.
Not a footprint or legacy will be left by the ungodly.
Their footsteps shall be removed,
and their voices of hatred will be buried in hell.

Epic 63

The Lord is my strength and my shield,
a shelter to those in need.

Protect me, O Lord, from the Wicked One.
Cover my soul and spirit with loving-
kindness and tender mercy.
Show clemency to those of a broken heart.

Father, reveal Yourself to the upright and
whisper soft, sweet music into my soul.
The sound of Your words and voice, O God,
brings such joy to my inner being.
My soul desires to be filled with a downpour of revelation.

Shower Your servant with grace.
Cover me in grace so that any storms
that try to overtake me will not prevail.
The gates of hell shall not triumph over me,
for I have the spirit and might of the living God.

Breathe into me unconditional favor, godly wisdom,
and an obedient spirit, O God,
for it is You I hunger for.
My spirit and soul thirst to be in Your presence for eternity.

O Lord, the Lord of heaven and earth, lead
Your servant into righteousness.
Keep my soul from wickedness.
Oh, how the brightness of the Majesty's Spirit
illuminates the darkness.
Darkness shall not prevail against You.

Keep my foot from falling into the traps of the Wicked One.
You are a God who sees and knows all.
A great and mighty God who no one can escape.
Preserve my soul and spirit even
when the hairs on my head turn snow white.
My Lord, You carried me in Your bosom when I was a child.
Even until old age You will still be my Father.

A Father for eternity who rescues His
children from the pit of destruction.
The pit of destruction is not meant for God's children.
The children of God were created to rule over the
earth and everything.

Wreak havoc and torment upon those who curse
Your people, Lord.
Shut the mouths of the wicked and soothsayers
who curse the righteous.
Send forth a deadly pestilence, Jehovah, to
the witches and warlocks.

As pestilence and curses from hell shall
overtake the wicked while in their graves,
the wicked believe they are invincible and own the world.
But His Royal Majesty has sovereignty
over the earth and planets.

You are a comforter and a father to those in distress.
To those who do evil, O God, You punish
them with a whip of sorrow and sadness.
When tears of sorrow and sadness cover the righteous,
the Lord turns the tears into joy.
Weeping may endure for a night but joy
comes in the morning. (Psalms 30:5)

Hosanna in the highest, flourish the earth
with milk and honey.
Show forth a sign of such great magnitude
that the idolaters will fall on their knees and
worship the true, living God.

You are a God who is faithful to Your promises.
The Father's promises are sacred words from His belly.
Flood the earth with Your presence, Father.

Fill this dark world with hope.
Show the world that Yahweh is a God
who will live for eternity.
Yahweh will annihilate the Antichrist in the blink of an eye.
The Lord's Spirit will continue to
hover over the universe after
Armageddon is complete.

Epic 64

As I sit in Your divine presence,
I sense the Holy One encamping around me.
As the waters rage upon the sands,
I know You control the currents in the sea.

The Majesty's presence is felt everywhere.
As I write to You, my Lord, the ocean and
the sea creatures bow at Your feet.
Breathe favor wisdom, might, valor, and power upon the lost.

Your Majesty, command the winds from the
north, south, east, and west to overtake the wicked.

You are always and forever in my heart.
Even when I sin against You, my Lord,
You are faithful to forgive Your servant.
Though some of us do degrading and immoral acts,
Your grace and unmerited forgiveness outweighs any sin
we have committed.

Give me a fresh start, O God.
Break the hand of Satan, my God, over the weak.
Remove the chains and shackles from the destitute.

Reveal Yourself, O God, to the world.
Show the world that the living God has a
power no foe can withstand.
Father, release Your glory from the heavens.

Jehovah, open the heavens with Your majestic hands.
Father, release Your glory from the heavens.

Jehovah, open the heavens with Your majestic hands.
Help us to call forth things as naught as though they were.
Send miracles from the heavens so the wicked may see
that You are an almighty God.

Shut the mouths of those who speak evil in Your sight.
Close the mouths of the Holy Rollers and hypocrites.
Crush and demolish the spirits of those
who hurt and taunt the poor.

The time shall come when we shall rule like gods.
We are made in the Father's image,
so let us live the life Christ has died for us to have.
Even though Christ suffered a brutal death,
He carries a legacy that shall remain even after Armageddon.

False teachers, leaders, and prophets
have perverted the sacred Word of God.
These people teach the world but have no love in their hearts.
False prophets wander the earth speaking untrue mysteries.

Father, reveal Your mysteries unto Your servant.
You hide Your mysteries in treasuries that no man can find.
The Lord treasures His sacred mysteries.

Satan thinks he knows the Father's hidden mysteries.
The Devil creates so-called mysteries and secrets
to make people believe in the "Big Secret."
Do not chase after so-called mysteries and prophecies
that are not of the Father.

Remove the soothsayers and haters who speak against You.
Bring forth a calamity upon those who
lead Your children astray.
Scatter whoremongers, sorcerers, witches,
warlocks, and idolaters to and fro the earth.

Those who speak evil of the Lord shall die by the sword.
The sword is imperious and can cut through anything.
The Word of God is sharper than any two-edged sword,
piercing between soul and spirit. (Hebrews 4:12)

Oh, good citizens of the Lord, use your mouth
to exterminate Satan and his fallen angels.
The forces of darkness are inferior
compared to the God we serve.
Your mouth is a ferocious weapon against the darkness.

Satan will throw darts, missiles, and curveballs to weaken us.
But the Lord has blessed us with something so powerful
that no devil can still our words.
Words can heal or destroy.
Choose to eradicate Satan with the Word!

Epic 65

Yahweh, save the lost who are in the darkness.
Pull the weak and dumfounded from the pit of destruction.
Satan and his angels are awaiting their death.

The unjust judge and his army desires your soul and spirit.
Everywhere you turn, the darkness follows you.
You were surrounded by darkness as an adolescent.

Your past haunts you.
You have done things to get ahead in life.
Sadness, hurt, and confusion have clouded your judgment.

If I die, where will my soul and spirit go?
The Lord knows my heart.
I often ask myself, "How will I die?
Will I die by the sword of Satan, or will I die a
peaceful death?"
Only the Father in heaven knows my beginning
to the end.

Epic 66

You are my lamp in a world filled with darkness and chaos.
You, O Lord, illuminate my paths so the
darkness does not overtake me.
You hide wisdom and knowledge for the righteous.

Cherish the wisdom the Master has bestowed upon you.
The Lord grants wisdom to all His children.
The wisdom the Lord grants is far
superior to human intelligence.

The Master hides His wisdom from the world
because it does not believe in the living God.
Why bless people with wisdom if they
are going to worship Baal?
The Devil lacks wisdom;
he knows that almighty God has a storm
that will soon eradicate him.

Guide the lost, brokenhearted, and depressed into the truth.
The world is filled with false lies and heretical doctrine.
Remove the false teachers from the podium, God.

These delusional teachers poison minds with lies.
These so-called pastors, teachers, and prophets of God
speak with such eloquence that one will fall for their lies.

Do not follow after those who appear to be Christ like
because they are intellectuals.
Guard your heart and mind from these wicked people.
Pray diligently so you will know when the Lord is speaking.

There are many creatures wandering this world
with Christ like qualities and demeanor,
but underneath the fancy attire and great intelligence
lies a demonic beast;
a demon from hell that craves the souls and spirits of people.

These people appear to be human,
but their souls and spirits are from hell.
Woe to you who forms heretical doctrine and
alters the sacred words of the Lord.
The time shall come when the wicked
shall consume their own lies.

Bring terror and pestilence upon those
who curse the righteous
and cause the wicked to drown in the lake of fire.

The righteous will never be forsaken.
You know the heart of mankind.
You search the soul and heart of man.
You, O God, know everything I do before I do it.

One cannot escape the Spirit of the Lord.
His Highness' Spirit hovers over the entire universe,
even in the darkest and most wicked places on earth.
Woe to you who think they can escape the Almighty.

His Majesty rides on chariots of fire.
He is clothes with wisdom, might, and valor.
The Lord causes the thunderstorms and the seas
to move at His command.

Thick cumulonimbus clouds cover the Lord's face.
No man, woman, or beast has ever laid eyes on the Great One.
Glory fills the earth as the Lord pours His Spirit on us.

Rain showers engulf us in Your glory, O God.
Rain wisdom, knowledge, intelligence,
and reverential fear of You.
Open the eyes and ears to those who do not know the truth.

What is truth?
The truth shall set you free. (John 8:32)
God is the way, the truth and the life. (John 14:6)

No more crying or sadness.
Everlasting peace and joy shall overtake you when
you are converted from darkness to light.
I am no longer a slave to the darkness.
My spirit has seen the light and the goodness of the Lord.

Epic 67

As long as there is breath within my spirit and soul,
I shall sing praises unto His Majesty.
You, O Lord, are the rock of my salvation.
In the midnight hour of distress, my spirit shall
still sing hymns and groans unto the Almighty.

Bless my soul, O God, for in Your presence is godly wisdom.
Hide Your servant from the pit of destruction.
Keep me under Your wing of protection.

You are a beacon to those in darkness,
a great and awesome God who reveals who we really are.
A father to those who are broken in spirit.

You restore life and longevity to the dying and distraught.
A magnificent God who rescues the righteous from
the hand of the adversary.
The adversary is a master manipulator of the sacred words
that Jehovah speaks.

Wisdom flows from Abba Father's belly
into His servant's spirit.
God, who is Spirit-filled, shields His children from harm.
Though Satan seeks our soul and spirit,
Yahweh made a sacrifice for us to have eternal life.

My spirit desires to be in the Almighty's presence,
for in the Almighty's presence is revelation,
knowledge, and wisdom.
Rubies and emeralds cannot compare
to the immense intelligence
of the Great One.

It is the Lord who blesses His children
with the reverential knowledge
and fear of Him.
Reveal Your hidden mysteries unto me, O God.
Revealing Yourself, O God, brings my soul and spirit
into everlasting peace.

You are the Prince of Peace.
The peace, my Lord, You have given me to withstand the
fiery darts of the Wicked One.
Though Satan and his angels are trying
to cause my ship to sink,
You have anchored me in Your Word.

Even though fiery darts, demons, and
sickness try to penetrate
my spirit and soul,
Yahweh has blessed me with the ability
to stare death in the face.
Things will attempt to pull me away from my Lord,
but His Word can never be annihilated.

Do not fall for the traps of the Wicked One.
Do not accept all prophecies, for everything spoken
must be tested and tried.
Not every prophecy is God-breathed.

Seek the Lord's face at all times.
Do not be misled by someone because they articulate
God's Word well,
for we are in a time of false teachers and prophets.

Listen and yearn for the presence of Yahweh.
Yahweh shall lead thee into all truth.
The Word of God is true and shall never fail you,
but the word of a false prophet shall
be cast into the pit of hell.

Believe the things the Lord your God has revealed
unto your spirit.
Do not fret in these last days, for imitators shall
pervert the truth and lead many astray.
But you, dearest child of God, have a bond that no
devil can rip apart.

Your Spirit, my Lord, shall dwell within me even
after Armageddon.
I am united in mind, soul, spirit, and body with Christ.
When I come home unto You, my Lord, I shall
live in Your bosom for eternity.

Epic 68

One must let go of the past to propel himself forward.
Call on the Lord Jehovah,
for He is a God who wipes away many tears.
Wrap me in Your arms, O God, for I long for You.

Help Your servant to preserve herself.
When I call on the Lord, He rescues me from my distress.
Many afflictions are of the righteous,
but the Lord delivers him out of them all. (Psalms 34:19)

Draw me near You, Holy Spirit.
Take me to that secret place where it is just me and You.
You are the love of my life.

A God that cherishes His people.
A King that adheres to His wife's every need.
Though Satan and his angels attempt to throw
daggers at my marriage,
it is Christ who keeps us together.

The Almighty is the fabric that keeps us united in
mind, body, soul, and spirit.
My husband and I have a sacred bond with His
Majesty that no creature of the night can destroy.

Preserve your body and soul for your husband.
You have called me into holy matrimony with
You before the foundation of the world.
A great husband, Lord, You are,
for You cherish me like rubies and emeralds.

You are the peace that covers my soul and spirit.
A God who breathes life and wisdom into
the brokenhearted.
My lips and hands shall continue to bless the Holy One,
for He is worthy.

Rain favor, wisdom, might, and valor upon Your servant.
I am forever Your most loyal and humble servant,
for Your love, O God, comforts my soul and spirit
during heartache.

When adversity comes upon me,
the Lord shall reach from on high and defeat
the forces of darkness.
Release the Master's people from bondage.
If you do not, may the Lord strike you with
a mighty blow.

The Lord's anger is so ferocious that one will
quiver in his soul.
Grant clemency to the lost, Father, for they have
been blinded by the Enemy.
Remove the scales and veil from the blind,
for they are in bondage.

Remove the false preachers and teachers from
Your sacred ground.
Remove the words from the mouths of
false prophets and witches.
You said, O God, that a witch shall not be spared.

Cloud the minds and judgment of the wicked,
for they shall wallow in constant chaos and confusion.
But You, O God, show mercy to those who are upright.
You show Yourself pure and loving to those who
seek redemption.

Though we sin, God, You have not banished us from
Your presence.
Far from good and pure we are.
But we serve a God that looks beyond the
physical;
He looks at our heart and inner man.

Epic 69

Bless be the name of our Father, who is in heaven.
Enter His gates with holy hands and a pure heart.
Worship the Lord God in the beauty of His essence.

You will find comfort and healing in His presence.
Joy fills my heart when You comfort my soul and spirit
in distress.
Make my paths clean, O God, so I may not depart from You.

Keep me in Your presence, Jehovah.
Cleanse my spirit and soul from all sin.
Banish those who do evil to the righteous, O God.

Give me the strength, Lord, to not dwell in the past,
for the things that occurred in the past are but
a mere shadow of what is to come.
The things that happened in the past have molded me
into the being I am.

Bless me with a spirit that is sensitive to Your sacred words.
Guide me into all truth, for You shall
not withhold any good thing.
Speak revelation, wisdom, and might into my spirit.
Guide my footsteps, Father, so I may not be deceived.

Bring Your servant into a deeper, intimate connection.
Shelter me under Your wing from all hurt.
Although You allow hurt to test me,
it does not crush my spirit.

Grant me a spirit to withstand all adversity.
No matter how much hell and persecution I must endure,
I shall put my trust in the Lord.

Breathe happiness, joy, peace, and laughter into me.
Reveal to the world, O God, that You are not a dead God,
but a God who lives for eternity.

Epic 70

I must let go to get to the Promised Land.
Help me, O God, so I do not push away the God-fearing
husband You have set before me.
Bind up and heal my wounded heart.

I desire to be with him
but if it is not Your will, Lord, remove the love
from my heart.
Cover him with Your wing, O God,
for he is lost in the darkness.

Gluttony has overtaken his spirit.
Reveal to his spirit that it is You who has preserved him.
Warn him of danger from the Enemy.

Reveal to him that Satan seeks his soul.
Reveal to him that Satan has many traps set for him.
Pull him from the shackles and chains.

Loose the yoke that is suffocating the inner man.
Reveal to him who he really is.
Release the Great On who dwells within him.

I pray that he will cry to You, Father.
Convict him in his spirit.
Revoke the death sentence,
for he has not completed his journey.
The Lord shall free him from the powers of darkness.

Fall on your knees and lift holy hands unto His Majesty.
Cleanse me from all unrighteousness,
for I have sinned before You.
Turn my mourning into joy,
for I am lost in the wilderness.

Convict me of my sins, O Lord, so I may walk in
Your ordinances.
Prick my heart.
Give me a heart that is pure and sensitive to Your voice.

Guide my soul into truth.
Reveal to me where I have sinned.
Remove the dark forces that have enslaved me to
the unjust judge.

I desire to do what is just and right.
But I often find myself indulging in acts that are
not of the Lord.
Both sides desire my soul.
Whom will I serve?
Will I serve God or mammon?

I desire the riches and abundant life of this world.
But what price must I pay to achieve greatness?
Will I do what is wrong to gain success,
or will I humbly submit thyself unto the Lord?
You choose.

Epic 71

Bless the name of the Lord forever and ever!
For wisdom, might, glory, and honor flows from
His belly.
Power flows from the Lord's Spirit unto His servants.

Praise the Lord night and day, for it honors Him.
Come before Him with clean hands and a tender heart.
My mouth shall continue to worship the Father,
even in times of adversity.

Fill the earth with Your magnificent glory.
Rain miracles, signs, and wonders on Your people.
Restore what was lost to the faithful.

Reveal unto Your servant what is to come.
You are a God who shall leave a legacy for centuries.
Times and season change, but the Lord never changes.

You are the same yesterday, today, and forevermore.
The Lord who rescues His people from the sword of Satan.

Though we get ourselves into trouble,
You are a father who still rescues us.
Though You chastise us with the rod of discipline,
You do it to turn us from our evil ways.

You discipline Your children out of love,
but to the wicked You release damnation.
It rains on the just and the unjust,
but the unjust shall have a continual downpour of rain.

The sun shines on the just and the unjust,
but the flames of the wicked shall soon go out.
The light of the uncompromising righteous gets
brighter and brighter,
but the lamp of the wicked shall soon burn out.

There are no lighted pathways in hell,
only utter darkness and chaos filled with lies and hatred.
But the righteous shall always have lighted paths,
for their spirits dwell with the Father.

Epic 72

You are a God who answers His servant in distress.
I cry unto my Lord, "Holy, holy,"
for You shall reign for eternity.
In Your presence is wisdom and fulfillment.

Peace, love, joy, happiness, and tranquility shall
cover me all the days of my life.
I shall cherish the Father's commandments and statutes.
Grace, wisdom, might, power, and honor clothe
His Majesty as He sits on the throne.

No false gods shall ever supersede the Holy One.
These carved, wooden gods stand with no life.
But the Lord has the power to breathe life into the dead.

There are many nomads among us wandering the streets,
preaching other hidden secrets.
These nomads spread deceit and lies.
These people are filled with such deceit that
Satan has blinded them into believing their false doctrine.

Superstitions and illusions consume the people.
Religious heretics, who appear to be godly,
but are detached from the truth.
Most trusted and loyal servant of the Lord,
hold fast to what the Father has spoken to you.

Bind upon your heart the truth God has instilled in you.
Do not be deceived by so-called followers of Christ.
Following these people will cause you to stray from the truth.

There are many other teachers out there and
other teachings that contradict the
sacred words of the Father.
But you shall you know them by their fruit. (Matthew 7:16)

Pastors from the Lord's own heart
fill God's people with words of inspiration and truth.
But false teachers and leaders use poisonous words
to blind the truth.
The Lord will expose their deception!

Do not pervert the sacred words of the Lord,
for if you do, the Lord shall curse you.
Do not prove or tempt the Lord.
The Lord shall not be made a mockery.
If you do, damnation and pestilence shall
follow you, even into your grave.

The Lord is gentle to those who are good-spirited.
But the Lord is like a tornado to those
who do evil in His sight.
Engulf the wicked, O God, in wrath that shall consume
them for eternity.

Cause a calamity to feed on the souls of those who
try to lead Your people astray.
A calamity that the world has dared not see.
You are the God of love but also the God of War.

You are the God of order but also the God of chaos
in the lives of the wicked.
Loving and caring to Your people
but vexing to the unrighteous.

Worship the Lord in the beauty of His essence.
Worship Him with a pure heart.
Continue to praise Him even while in the
fiery furnace or staring death in the face,
for the Lord is faithful to deliver His people.

While stones, darts, and swords may get thrown at me,
I know that God has given me a weapon
no devil can withstand.
A sword and mouth that will bring many to their knees.

I have a fire within me that shall never burn out.
A fire that gets hotter as I get closer to God.
A fire that will burn anything that is wicked.

Epic 73

You are a great and awesome God who is to be praised.
The God of my strength, my high
tower in whom I take refuge.

You are my rock, O God, in whom I trust and rely.
Salvation and grace have encamped about me.
Unconditional love, kindness, and tender mercies
shall follow me all days of my life.

I will forever love my Father, for He has breathed life into me.
You are the author and finisher of my life.
You shall direct my paths and lead me into righteousness.

You are the hope I cling to.
You give hope to the hopeless.
Those who are lost in the dark world, Lord,
You pull into the light.

Send forth Your bright light, O God,
so the world may see that You still reign.
Eradicate the forces of darkness with Your mighty sword.
Rip out the tongue and break the teeth of the wicked.

Cleanse this world, Father, from
iniquity and unrighteousness.
The people are crying for manifestations of the Lord.
Healing, wisdom, and supernatural
strength shall overtake the church.

Upon this rock shall I build my church,
and the gates of hell shall not prevail.
In these last days, the church shall be
a dynamic, unstoppable force.
Immovable and unshakeable shall God's people be.

Do not be terrified to go into dark, desolate places,
for the Lord shall be with you.
Though Satan has a mighty army,
the Father has an army that obliterates a nation.

Send forth a dark and murky pestilence to
those who dishonor and disobey You, Master.
The Creator of good and bad.
The Creator of heaven and hell.
The Creator of Jesus and Satan.

For You, O Lord, hold the entire universe and
all human beings in Your hand.
In Your hand, Father, lies the keys to heaven and hell.

You have written and formulated how
my life is going to turn out.
Many people have decided how my life is going to be.
But You, Lord, have the final word
and judgment upon my life.

God uses the foolish to confound the wise.
You have taken me, Father, where people
think I cannot achieve greatness.
I thank You, Father, for instilling Your dreams into my spirit.

Weak and timid I used to be.
But the Lord has hardened me like sharp iron
so when Satan attack me with his weapons,
they will ricochet from my sword and
pierce him in the spirit.

Sweet and gentle to the weak I am but a
ferocious and ravenous lion toward the wicked.

Epic 74

Make a joyful noise unto the Lord.
Praise His mighty name, for it is He who gives precious life.
God breathed His magnificent Spirit into our bodies
so we may have everlasting life.

The Lord guides our footsteps even when it
appears we are going in the wrong direction.
The Father is with us even during our darkest seasons.
There is no escaping the Great One,
for His Spirit hovers over the entire universe.

You were there, God, when you called me into existence.
My Lord, You will be there on day of judgment
when I stand before You.
You will judge many, O God, including the nations and
their leaders.

From the small insects that roam in the dirt
to the kings of nations,
Your eyes have watched them.
No one has been able to escape the eyes of the Lord.
If you hide from Him, the Lord shall expose you.

Comfort the nations, O God.
The people of the nations cry unto You, my Lord,
for a downpour of Your Spirit.
Engulf the earth with Your glory and wisdom.

Turn the wicked from their hideous ways.
Make Satan crawl into the cave of cowardice.
Power lies in the words of good citizens of God.

Release Your wrath, Father, on those who do heinous acts.
Cause the sorcerers, witches, and other so-called spiritualists
to eat the curses they have sent forth unto the just.
The just shall live by faith, (Hebrews 10:38)
but the evildoers of the night shall be cast unto the dogs.

Epic 75

I will forever give His Majesty praise and honor.
Honor the Lord your God with all that is within your heart.
Praise the Lord,
for when you do virtue flows from Him unto you.

Praising God opens many doors.
When we give the Father praise during the night seasons,
it makes Satan quiver.
Satan despises giving God praise
because in praising the Lord comes strength and virtue.

Strength, might, valor, virtue, and excellence
are clothed in the Father's Spirit.
In His presence is the fulfillment of desire.
Saturate me with Your presence, O God.

Peace and tranquility shall cover me.
A peace, O God, that transcends all understanding.
An unshakeable peace you have bestowed upon me.

You are a God of order and justice.
A God who supersedes all natural intelligence and strength.
The Lord of heaven and earth.

The Creator of humans, inventions, and other species.
No other god can match the might nor do miracles
like Jehovah-Jireh.

There is power in Your name, O God.
When pagan worshippers call upon their false gods,
they have no power to deliver them.
But when You call on the Lord,
He will deliver you speedily.
For our Lord is gracious and Father to those in distress.

When I am in distress, Father, You wipe my tears.
Though tears of gloom stream down my face,
You comfort me.
Though I cannot see the face of the living God,
His presence comforts and consoles my spirit.

Do not run into the arms of the so-called spiritualists
and so-called true prophets of the Lord in times of turmoil,
for these people speak futile prophecies.
Consult the Lord in all your ways and He
will lead your paths. (Proverbs 3:5)

There are many wandering prophets among
the children of God.
Not every prophesy is God-breathed.
Test every word that person has spoken.

Do not allow imitators to rob you of the precious Word
that God has instilled in you.
The Father knows these imitators.
Do not be dismayed when a demon of the night,
dressed in sheep's clothing, tries to lead you astray
or speaks some unknown tongue.

For the Lord knows every language that is spoken
and the hidden words.
Devils speak in unknown tongues too,
but the Lord will reverse their demonic words.
The Father is an immovable and irrevocable force.

The forces of God are more robust than the
forces of darkness.
Though we may be surrounded by darkness,
the Father is a beacon on dark paths.

Do not fear dark and desolate places.
Though Satan may appear as a mighty spirit,
the Lord has given us a weapon to destroy him.

Do not battle Satan in human strength,
for you cannot defeat him in that manner.
Use your words, which are like fire to ward off evil.
Evil despises good works of the Lord,
but the Almighty has a Spirit that can ravage a nation.

Nations battling nations,
children rebelling against parents,
and the evildoers indulging in unrighteousness.
Even though unrighteousness consumes
the earth,
you good citizens of the God hold fast to your
confession of faith.

The earth belongs to His Majesty,
for He is the Creator of all.
All living beings are subject to the Lord,
even the wicked beings of the night.

We must all give an account unto the Lord.
Do what is right and just, even when it is painful.
The Lord knows the heart of man, which is deceitful.
Cleanse me, O God, from all unrighteousness
so I may stand at Your feet.
Uncleanness and unrighteousness do not dwell in
the house of the Lord.

Epic 76

Give praises and blessings unto His Majesty!
Make a joyful noise unto the Lord!
Sing praises and hymns to the Father,
for He is the rock and strong tower of our salvation!

You are the King of Kings and Lord of Lords.
You are a mighty King who comforts His people.
A loving, gentle, and caring God.

You ride on Your chariots of fire,
vindicating those who have been put to shame.
Shame shall not cover me, for You, O God,
will clothe me in Your grace.
Your grace is everlasting.

Clothe me in Your magnificent presence.
Saturate my soul and spirit with wisdom,
for wisdom is far superior to rubies and riches.

Yea, though I desire the riches and lavish life
of the temporal world,
I desire the richness of God's Spirit and joy.
Joy comes in the morning,
but joy can also come in the midnight hour.

I cried and shouted unto the Lord to
deliver me from my adversities.
Though I wept for help,
the Lord gave me His grace and strength to endure.
Though the fires of hell may surround my soul,
the fire shall never penetrate my spirit.

The fires of Satan may set you ablaze,
but the Father will not allow it to put you in the grave.
You are a walking testimony to the trials and
tribulations the Wicked One has sent forth.
But, my dear child, the Lord did not allow Satan
to take you asunder.

You will endure pain, heartache, and disappoints in this life,
but the Lord shall give you strength to persevere
through the fires of hades on this earth.
Earth is only a temporal home,
for your spirit resides in the kingdom of heaven.

Epic 77

Peace, blessings, glory, and power be unto Him
who sits on the throne.
The Lord's throne is everlasting,
but the throne of a tyrannical monarchy
shall be overthrown.

The Lord decides who will be king.
He sets up kingdoms for a purpose.
But the Father has the authority to
strip a king of his sovereignty.

Do not allow Satan to get you to be
prideful, arrogant, and boastful of your great works.
It is the living God who has allowed you
to get wealth and prestige.

Oh, how I want great wealth, riches, and recognition.
But we forget that God has the power
to bring us to our knees.
Do not forget the Lord your God who has blessed you
with all gifts, including spiritual gifts.

These spiritual gifts the Father has bestowed upon us
are to guide us and aid others.
Do not manipulate others with your spiritual gifts
or the Lord will judge you.

Judge the godless nations, O Lord, for
they do wickedness in Your sight.
The ungodly nations chastise those
who revere and worship You.
The godless nations shall suffer the wrath of the Lord.

Lord, bless those who walk upright within
Your statutes and ordinances.
Keep the Lord's statutes,
for they will help you in times of distress.

You cause the heavens to open at Your command.
The angels and the cherubs bow at Your feet.
His Excellency causes the angels and the heavens
to move on our behalf.

Move on the behalf of Your people, O God.
Cause a downpour of unbelievable and never seen miracles.
Cause the sick, the lame, and the dumb to be healed
before the people.

The dumb shall speak of the goodness of the Lord.
The sick shall be healed and give praise unto His Majesty.

Sing and make a joyful noise unto the Lord.
Enter into His courts with an open heart
and a thankful spirit,
for the Lord deserves to be magnified and praised.

Magnify the Lord.
Give praise to the Father even when it appears
Satan is winning.
In times of vexation, the Lord shall be a comforter unto you.

Comfort Zion, for she is weeping.
Purge the earth of her sins.
Cleanse and crucify those who Satan has in captivity.

Satan desires us to be captive,
but the Lord paid a precious price for our freedom.
Free we are from the pit of destruction,
and free you are in the presence of the Lord.
May the Lord be with you.

Epic 78

Holy is the Lord my God.
Clean and pure are the Lord's hands,
for the Lord touches no unclean thing.
Holiness, grace, and valor encamp around His Majesty.

Majestic are Your wings.
Your wings, O God, extend from the heavens.
Beautiful You are, my Lord.

My Lord, extend your kindness and comfort the needy.
You clothe the poor with loving-kindness
and tender mercies.
Yahweh, the Lord of my strength.

You are the peace that I hold dear.
A peace to those who are banished and exiled
from the world.
In a world of chaos, You still hold the universe
in the palms of Your hands.

The Father's belly is filled with hidden mysteries,
hidden secrets that are stored and revealed
unto Your servants.
Servants of kings come and go,
but a true servant of the Lord holds dear to the King of Kings.

There are many kingdoms set upon this earth,
but Jehovah's kingdom shall never be removed.
Every king is born for an appointed time,
but the King of Glory is the king for eternity.

Monarchies come and go,
but the kingdom of God shall never be defeated.
The God we serve is immortal.

Mortal we may be,
but we serve a God who has reversed the death sentence.
Though we die a physical death,
our spirits shall live for eternity.

Our spirits will roam to and fro the earth and in the heavens.
The Spirit of the Lord shall engulf those who seek His face.
His face we cannot touch or see,
but the Father's presence is felt throughout many nations.

Many nations cry, "Abba Father!"
for the people desire to be filled with
the Almighty's presence.
The presence of the Lord bring us into an
intimate and deep understanding of Him.
Though the world disregards God and His mysteries,
we servants of the Lord have been
blessed to know His secrets.

The Lord hides His mysteries from man.
The Lord cherishes His secrets and
reveals them to the true believer.

Many so-called secrets are loose in this world.
So-called secrets have perverted the
things God spoke and fought for.
But the day shall come when the Lord shall shut the mouths
of these imposters and cast their secrets into hell.

These secrets shall be locked in the cases of hell.
The mouths of the wicked shall be sealed along with
their venomous words.
Not a sound from their voices shall be heard on earth.

Epic 79

Love the Lord with all your heart, mind, body, and soul.
The Lord's voice is peaceful like a summer breeze.
The Almighty's presence is comforting
like the sound of ocean waves.

Breathe favor, might, and wisdom in my direction.
Cover me under Your majestic wings.
Your wings, O God, are a shield to those who Satan desires.

Satan is a pervert and an imposter of God's Word.
Though Satan tries to destroy the sacred words of the Father,
the he cannot destroy what the Lord has ordained.

The Lord has called many things and beings into existence.
Whatever Jehovah has created shall never be exterminated,
for the Father in heaven has a purpose for everything.

Seasons and purpose are implanted into the earth.
Winter, summer, spring, and fall are
commanded from the heavens.
The heavens are filled with God's omnipotent power.

El Shaddai causes the heavens and earth
to shake at His command.
Fill the earth with Your glory, O God.
Saturate the people with Your Spirit.
The Spirit of the Lord moves in ways unnatural to man.

Man rationalizes how God operates.
But mankind is detached from God's Spirit,
so he roams in the darkness, seeking
answers to the unknown.
Every answer is not in a textbook.
Some answers are God-breathed and hidden for the just.

The just shall live by faith,
but the wicked shall be cut off and banished from
the Lord's presence.
The Lord's presence is pure.
No unclean thing shall dwell in Him

Cleanness, purity, and sanctification
dwell in the Father's sight.
The Father's belly is filled with many
ideas and great inventions.
Intelligence, wisdom, and glory encamp around His throne.

The Lord's throne is secure forever.
No other gods shall supersede Him.
The Father's throne was established and secure
before He called Adam into existence.

We serve a God who has undeniable power and strength.
His strength is made perfect in our weakness.
Where weakness dwells comes the
inner strength of the Father.

Mighty You are, O God.
A king who is loyal to His subjects.
A king who would ravage another kingdom.

A kingdom that has no boundaries or limits.
A profound, limitless God we serve.
A king whose monarchy shall leave
footprints on many nations.

Epic 80

The Father knows that I, His daughter,
have endured tumultuous times.
I have had opposition from the moment
I stepped foot into my destiny.
I am destined for greatness and called to
be at one with the Father.

My heart is pure and tender toward You, O God.
You are the husband I have desired since I was a youth.
A husband who will never leave nor forsake His wife.

A great friend You are, O God.
A great listener and comforter.
You comfort me through the midnight hour
in times of distress.

A lover to those in need.
A comforter to the brokenhearted.
A father who will fight for justice.

I will dance with the Father into eternal bliss.
A sacred and spiritual marriage we have, O Lord.
The Lord of my life and the Lord who rules over
many nations.

A mighty and just God You are.
A God who ravages and clothes the wicked in darkness.
The Lord who commands the ocean and the seas to stop.

You give life to the trees and plants.
A giver and treasurer of life,
You have breathed Your Spirit into me, O God,
so the world may know You are alive.
Clothe my spirit and soul with righteousness
and tender mercy.
Instill to me the knowledge and strength of my forefathers.
Breathe Your glory from the heavens onto Your people.

Fill the earth with glory and everlasting peace.
Cover the earth with Your magnificent presence.
The presence of the Lord shall be felt
after humanity is extinct.

Many will be touched by the presence of God.
Many will hear and see that the God we serve is powerful.

Even though wood-carved gods appear majestic,
they lack might and ability to perform miracles.
These wooden gods just stand without life.
But our Father in heaven manifests Himself
in ways that our eyes and minds cannot comprehend.

A pagan god can be of no assistance in times of pain
and heartache.
But the Lord God Almighty comes on high and
gives us strength to go on.
A strength no devil can withstand.

The Lord is hovering over the universe continuously.
His eyes are in places we cannot see.
He uses us, His vessels, to complete His will.
A will done by few but felt by many.

Epic 81

You are the master of my fate, O God.
You lead me into my divine destiny and purpose.
Everyone has a purpose and a destiny,
but some may never find their true calling.

You, my Lord, have instilled dreams and creativity
into my spirit.
My spirit longs to see the richness and fullness of Your Word
manifested across many nations.
My spirit and soul desires to see Your Majesty's glory
spread throughout the earth.

Manifest Yourself, O God, to the nations.
Show Yourself strong, my Lord, in the
presence of unbelievers.
Demonstrate to the world that You are not dead
but the Sovereign Lord, Ruler, and Jehovah that breathes
life into dead and desolate places.

Wreak havoc and calamity upon those
who curse the Lord God.
Breathe a detrimental fire upon those who slay Your people.

Send forth fire to the ungodly nations
for persecuting Your people.
Inject a mighty wind into the saints so people may know
Your people are called.
Many are called but few are chosen. (Matthew 22:14)

Chosen ones of the Lord,
conduct yourselves like the Father.
The Father receives glory when His
children reflect His image.
Reign forever, my Lord, for You reign on high.

Your kingdom is eternal and everlasting, O God.
You are the ruler and Lord over heaven.
You are the Lord I shall cherish and
adore even unto my grave.

I will sing praises and hymns unto His Majesty.
His Majesty shall live and rule forever.
Eternally you shall live, O God,
for the angels, cherubs, and seraphims
encamp around the Father's throne.

Pure You are, my Lord, in all Your ways.
No unclean thing dwells in Your presence.
In His presence is the richness and
fullness of the Lord's Word.
The Lord's words are dynamic and filled with fire
that will pierce through any being.

There is a fire ablaze within my spirit and soul.
A fire that no demon in hell can withstand.
A fire that only desires to be quenched by the water
of the Holy Spirit.

The Holy Spirit is a ravaging fire for the Lord of Hosts.
His Majesty is calling me to more intimate levels.
A level that the Father and I encamp and dwell together.

Dwell in the Father's presence,
for in it you shall find peace, love, joy, happiness,
and fruits of the Spirit.
Clothe me with Your presence, fill me with everlasting glory,
and a peace that shall saturate me even unto my death.

When I go to be with the Father in heaven,
I shall leave a legacy unto mankind.
A legacy that shall be felt and leave footprints imprinted
on the hearts of men.
Respect His Majesty and His servant,
for when you do, the Lord shall recompense you.

Epic 82

I often question my intelligence.
A large part of me is at war with Satan.
Pessimistic thoughts constantly cover my soul.

My mind is clouded with preconceived ideas of failure,
for I do not know what life holds for me.
I have been quarreling with opposing forces
since I was an adolescent.

At times I would contemplate and ask myself,
"Is it meant for me to achieve what is in my heart?"
I try diligently not to revert to my old self.

For though I question the things the Lord my God does,
I know that everything happens for a reason.
I desire to know why certain things occur.
I know that sometimes the Father
will not give me the answer.

There is an answer behind every trial and tribulation,
but my soul and spirit must come to terms that
everything is not going to be answered.

I desire not to be moved and affected
by the things of this world.
My soul and spirit long to have the strength of the Lord,
for in times of distress, my soul aches.

My biggest fear is failure and not achieving greatness.
My spirit yearns to ascend like an eagle.
An eagle soars over every bird and is not affected
by the wind shifts.

Despite the winds and the storms that occur,
the eagle still remains on high.
In my heart, I long to be the best aviator.

I have always been the underdog,
and the winds have always been contrary.
I have become immune to the disappointments in life.

One does not know what life holds for them.
You never know what has been written
in the book for your life.

We have all been given a deck of cards,
and some have been given a bad deck.
Regardless of the cards I have,
I must learn to play the hand I have.

Though I may disagree with certain things,
God does as He pleases.
I will respect the Master,
for it is He who has breathed His Spirit and life into me.

I must be content and come to terms that
in life I will encounter failure.
Regardless of the outcome, I will accept
whatever comes into my path,
for it is God who controls the universe.

Epic 83

Lord guide me into all truth,
for it is You who is guiding my footsteps
into my God-given destiny.
Light the dark paths, O God, so I may see the opposing forces.

Illuminate my steps with Your omnipotent presence.
Cause Your presence from on high to saturate my spirit.
Fill my spirit and soul with the strength
and might of Your Word.

Your Word, O God, brings forth light
into dark and desolate places.
The Word of God brings healing and
health to the brokenhearted.
Once the Word of God penetrates through one's spirit,
it reconstructs one's identity and purpose.

Purpose and fulfillment come with
fellowship with the Father.
The Father desires an intimate
relationship with His children.
The Lord is a listener and a comforter to those in dire need.

Enter into the Father's presence with a thankful heart.
Come to Him like a tender child who desires the
unconditional love and affection of a parent.
The Lord is a parent to all who seek Him.

Seek the Lord with all your heart,
for in Him is the richness and fullness of His presence.
Cover me in wisdom, my Lord,
for when I speak the world shall know that it is You.

Speak and guide my mouth, O Lord.
Speak the truth to many nations so Your
Word will penetrate their souls.
Penetrate the hearts, souls, and spirits
of those who do not believe.

Arise, O warriors and great citizens of God.
Stand to the calling the Lord has placed within your spirit.
Spirit of the Lord, lead me to that place
of righteousness and holiness.

His Holiness is a father to the brokenhearted
and an avenger for the just.
Righteousness, tranquility, and peace
encamp around the Father.
Live and breathe to be imitators of His Majesty.
Do not forsake the covenant God has bestowed upon you.

Blessed are those who take refuge in the Lord.
Count it joy when the evildoers attack you,
for it is the power of the almighty God that rests upon you.

Joyful is the one who bears his cross for Christ.
Go out of the way for Christ.
As you adore and cherish Christ, He shall put you on a
pedestal for the nations to see.

Epic 84

Love the Lord your God with all your heart, mind, and soul.
Guard you heart with all vigilance,
for out of it flows the issues of life. (Proverbs 4:23)
Enter the Father's courts with a tender heart
and an attitude of appreciation.

The Father's belly is filled with wisdom,
knowledge, and intelligence.
Wisdom and the Spirit of truth engulf the Lord's being.
His throne is surrounded by power and fire.

The throne is good, pure, and free from all sin.
Come boldly to His throne,
for in it is the truth that you shall find everlasting life.
Everlasting life is what the body of Christ desires.

Desire to be at peace with one another.
Do not strive with those who do you wrong.
Allow the almighty God to scare them.

Do not allow anger to get the best of your soul and spirit.
Be at peace within your soul and spirit.
Do not allow the wicked to frazzle you.

The wicked receive glory when we fall for the traps of Satan.
Pray that Abba Father opens your spiritual
eyes and ears to His truth.
There are many so-called truths and theologies amidst,
but do not be led into the nonsense of other spiritual debates.

There is only one way, one truth, and one life.
That way is through Christ Jesus.
Christ Jesus is the only truth to get to God.

There is no side or back door into heaven.
One must accept and believe that Christ died.
He is Lord.

No other lord or god shall have dominion over the Father.
The Father has sovereignty over every being and creature.

Do not bow down or worship any false gods,
for when you do, the Lord your God
shall remove His presence.
Do not tempt or provoke the Lord your God.

Our God is great and greatly to be respected.
Respect the Creator who has breathed life into mortal souls.
He is the giver of life and the master of the universe.

It is the almighty God who holds our destiny
in the palms of His hands.
He decides our fate, not mankind.

Mankind is weak and foolish in the eyes of the Lord.
Do not listen to the venomous words of man,
for they will steer you into the pit of corruption.

Do not doubt the Lord your God.
Believe in Him and all His mysteries that He has revealed
unto your spirit.

Mankind lies, steals, kills, and destroys our being,
but the Lord has come to restore what is broken or lost.

Ignore the voices of the Enemy.
Believe in that still voice within your Spirit.
There are many deceitful spirits among us.
Which will you believe?
Believe in the Spirit of truth,
for in Him lies the keys of truth and destiny for your life.

Epic 85

Guide me into all truth so I am not misled by the Tempter.
The Tempter is a mischievous beast that spreads venom
into the lives of saints.
Saints, hold steadfast to the confession of your faith.

Do not be deceived by those who appear to godly.
Many imposters roam the world seeking out weak
and malnourished Christians.
Do not allow these false teachers to
impress you with great speech.

Every word must be tried and tested.
Everyone who says he believes in Christ
does not necessarily have a pure heart pure toward God.

Be vigilant, O saints of God, because
there is roaring lion a loose.
Everyone's heart is not pure and tender.
Do not be quick to believe the prophecy
of someone who is misleading.

Many seek stardom and prestige because
of the unfulfillment of the Lord.
These people do not have a yearning passion for God
or a relationship with Him.
These religious fanatics do it to gain
the respect of the people.

On the day of judgment, you shall be held accountable
for heretical doctrine that was spread throughout the land.
Believe only the words the Father has spoken into your spirit.

Believe in, adhere to, and trust the Spirit of truth,
for the Word of the Lord cannot lie!
Mankind lies, but the Father's sacred words are filled
with fire and truth.

Jehovah shall not lead you astray, my child.
He has ordained you to be prosperous
in mind, body, and soul.
Our lives are predestined and written in the
Lamb's Book of Life to have eternal life.

Eternal life with the Father in heaven
is what my spirit thirsts for.
Thirst for the fullness and richness
of the wisdom in His belly.
Abba Father's belly is filled with insight,
knowledge, wisdom, and
revelation that the natural man lacks.

Strive to be like the Lord.
Mimic the Lord in all His ways.
Be a representative of Christ,
for then people will see the living God within you.

Honor, worship, and praise unto His Excellency.
Valor, might, and strength clothe the
Almighty as He rides from on high.
Clouds of thunder and fire encamp around His throne.

Many kingdoms have been established upon the earth.
Kingdoms war over sovereignty,
but His Majesty has a kingdom that shall never be
ravaged by vandals.

Other kings have fallen by the sword of other monarchies.
The sword of a king holds dominion and might.
But we serve a King whose sword lives for eternity,
and His sword shall be imprinted on the hearts of men.

Many shall perish by the sword and
vexations of the Wicked One,
but good citizens of the Lord, hold fast
and guard your strength.
You shall need strength and might to
fight the good fight of faith.

Inject Your people, O God, with a ferocious fire
that will shake the nations.
Stir up and excite those sleeping nations.

Invade the earth, O God, with a supernatural force
that shall be remembered for centuries.
Decades and centuries have passed and times
have metamorphosed,
but the Lord is the same yesterday, today, and forevermore.
A God whose Spirit was the same when He
called forth the cosmos into existence.

Epic 86

I will adhere to You, my Lord, through the
good and bad.
My spirit shall especially cleave to the Almighty
during times of pandemonium.
During the tumultuous times on earth,
my spirit and soul shall continue to exalt the Creator.

There will always be a war between good and evil.
Satan will try to ravage the people of God
along with the kingdom of heaven.
But the almighty God has a might that encamps
around His Spirit.

The Lord's Spirit is filled with many wondrous works
that man knows nothing of.
The Father hides those precious secrets within His heart.
He stores the hidden mysteries for true followers.

True servants and worshippers of the Lord,
continue to strive to be at peace with one another.
Do not quarrel among each other,
for it causes division within the kingdom.
Be at peace within yourselves and make amends.

Strive for unity within the kingdom of God.
Do not be imitators of those who seek after the flesh.
Rather seek and inquire of the wisdom,
knowledge, and revelation
that is within the Father's belly.

Get to know the Father's heart.
Have a deep longing to knows the
Lord's ways and ordinances.
Bind upon your heart the ordinances
and statutes of the Lord.

O Lord in heaven, fill me with the reverential knowledge
and fear of You.
You are the Lord who determines and ordains my steps.
The God who predestined me to have
an intimate relationship
with Him.

Jehovah, You reign over all.
You have dominion over the universe,
the stars, and the cosmos.
The cosmos and fish of the sea move at Your command.

The voice of the Father brings comfort to my soul and spirit
during the midnight hour.
Even in your most nebulous and murky moments,
believe in the Lord your God with all your heart and soul.

Fill those whose spirits have been broken, O God.
Restore believers with a faith that can withstand
the fiery furnace.
Though the furnace is ablaze with a devastating fire,
believe that Jehovah will deliver you.

Though Satan tries to tempt me with the lust of life,
I will not forsake the One who breathed
life into my mortal body.
In times of utter distress, my fire
shall not extinguish but will
burn for eternity,
for it is the Word of God that keeps my spirit ablaze.

Epic 87

You are my Savior, O God,
for it is You who saved me from eternal damnation.
You broke the yoke from around my spirit and soul.

I was a slave to the Wicked One,
but Satan shall no longer have dominion over me,
for the almighty God has given me the ability to
tread upon all evil.

I shall fear no evil thing,
for the Lord has instilled in me a wrath no demon
can withstand.
A wrath that shall consume any wicked thing.

Preserve me, O God, from worldly affairs.
Preserve me and keep me pure for You, my Lord.
Help me keep my focus and attention on the prize
that is ahead of me.

I shall guard my heart with all vigilance,
for out of it springs the issues of life.
Help me guard and bridle my tongue, O God,
so I may not speak against You.

Keep me level-headed so I may not veer onto
the path of destruction.
The path of hades is awaiting those who delight
in doing evil.
Though we are surrounded by a world
filled with dark images,
our souls and spirits are at rest with the Father in heaven.

Fill me with Your presence, O God.
My spirit longs and thirsts for Your return.
The Lord's return will be felt by those across the nations
and by those in their graves.

The sick shall be healed.
The lame shall walk.
The blind shall see the wonders of the Lord.
The deaf shall hear the ordinances of the Lord.

Many signs and wonders shall consume the earth.
The earth shall be saturated with the goodness
and glory of the Lord.

His Majesty reigns on high.
His kingdom is not of this world and shall never perish
at the hands of the Wicked One.
The Wicked One is cursed for eternal damnation.

Wisdom and might are His.
In the Lord, you shall find purpose and the calling of life.
Oh, how precious life can be!

You are the giver and taker of life.
Life was created to imitate the Most High God.
Mimic the Lord in His ways.

Cover me, O Lord, under Your majestic wing.
Your wings have covered me from the fiery darts
of the Wicked One.
The Lord is a high, strong tower and refuge to those
in distress.

Distress and adversity shall not overtake my spirit,
for I have a devastating fire within my spirit that will
obliterate any opposition.

Though we may experience opposition
and the winds are contrary,
grab hold of the Lord's hand.
The almighty God has a firm and mighty hand.
The hand of the Father is gentle yet can cause
catastrophic winds that will be felt into the next millennium.

Catastrophic storms, tornadoes, hurricanes, and other
unexplained activity shall occur,
but the Lord in heaven shall protect His people.
No evil thing, entity, or fatal storm shall overtake you.

Adhere and hold fast to the things Abba Father
has revealed unto your spirit.
There are many spirits loose in the earth,
but the Lord is Creator over all.

Though these seductive spirits appear dynamic,
our Sovereign Lord controls these entities.
Do not be overtaken by evil.
Allow the Spirit of God to overtake and flow through
your innermost being.

Epic 88

For the Lord God is more mighty and powerful
than any foe upon earth.
The earth trembles at the Father's presence.
His omnipotent presence and strength
shall saturate my spirit.

The earth is the Lord's and all that is in it.
Earth was created to manifest the goodness of the Lord.
Lord, fill me with all wisdom and
knowledge within Your belly.

Reveal Yourself, O God, to the unbelieving and unfaithful.
Restore the lost with unshakeable faith.
Rejuvenate those who have been wounded in spirit and soul.

Replenish the weak with the strength of an eagle.
Crucify and burn the wretched spirit that wreaks havoc
on the just.
The just shall live by faith,
but the evildoers of the night shall perish by the sword.

Breathe everlasting strength into the brokenhearted.
Restore the years that the cankerworm
and locust have eaten.
Obedient children we are, honoring our Father in heaven.

Reward Your faithful servant in the open to the nonbelievers
and naysayers.
Shut the mouths of those who curse You in secret.
Pray in secret so the Lord your God may reward you openly.

Do not disclose to everyone your secret thoughts and prayers.
Do not reveal to everyone your dreams and ambitions,
for everyone is not on the same path as you.

Be careful, dear child of the Lord,
for there are wild scavengers among us.
Hold the precious words to your heart that Abba Father
has spoken unto your spirit.

Not everyone who speaks highly of His Majesty is of the Lord.
Test and try the words from the mouths of people.

Though these people appear warmhearted and God-fearing,
their spirit man is filled with loathsome and wicked things.
Do not be quick to accept the prophecies and words
from others into your spirit,
for there are many false spirits loose in the world.

We are in a world filled with hopelessness and despair.
The people are grasping and reaching for hope.
Hope and joy are no longer the centerfold in people's lives.

The chaotic and demonic world in which we reside
is filled with anger, hatred, and lust.
The spirits of greed, strife, and egocentrism have covered
the minds, souls, and spirits of people.
A dog-eat-dog world and covetous society we have become.

But you, dearest child of the Most High God,
continue to be humble and of a pure heart.

Do not allow the heretical methodologies and ideologies
deter you from the true living God.
Believe in the Creator who formed you into His image.

In His bosom is the fulfillment and joy of His majesty.
We serve a King who reigns and sits on high.
The Lord is too pure and great to be in the midst of swine.

The swine and the uncleanness of the
night shall dwell in hades.
But you, most trusted servant of the Lord, shall dwell in
peace and sanctification.
Consecrate yourself before the Lord.

Purify yourself before the Lord.
Root up and destroy the seeds that Satan has planted
within your soul and spirit.

Lord, cleanse and rejuvenate my broken spirit so
I may be a living will and testament to those in the
fiery furnace of hell.

Epic 89

Fall onto your knees and worship the Lord your God
in the beauty of His essence.
There is beauty, peace, joy, and meekness in the
Lord's presence.
Fill me, O Lord, with everlasting peace, joy, and tranquility.

You are holy and beautiful, O God,
for no other god is superior to You.
You are the Holy of Holies, and other false gods
or pagan idols cannot compare.
No being or entity is pure like His Majesty.

Purity, holiness, and sanctification
dwell in the Father's presence.
His presence is filled with omnipotent power and glory.
Glory, honor, and valor covers the throne of the Lord.

His throne is secure for eternity and shall never perish
at the hands of vandals.
We serve a God whose kingdom is not of this world
but rather an invisible realm that only
believers have access to.

Access the Father's presence through faith.
Worship and praise the Most High God.
Through prayer and supplication we gain knowledge
and reverential fear of His Majesty.

Do not fear the Lord your God,
for He is slow to anger.
He is a gentle God to those who are of a melancholy spirit.
He is gentle, meek, and soft-spoken to the lost and wounded.

Though you may be wounded in spirit and soul, my child,
reach unto the Comforter.
He comforts those who are broken in
mind, body, soul, and spirit.
The spirit man can be quite hazardous to the soul
because it harbors and carries the emotional
trials and tribulations one must endure in life.

The spirit man has to be purged and burned so the Lord
can make a new creation.
Holding onto past traumas and hurts can wound one in
mind, body, and soul.

The spirit man is like a video and tape recorder,
recording the good and evil.
Dear child of the Lord, do not hold onto the past.
Come into the Lord's presence like a child who is in
need of his Father.

Come, O Lord, and inject Your sovereign Spirit into
my weakened and broken spirit.
My spirit and soul desire to be whole
and at one with the Father.
Wholeness and completeness will saturate my soul and
surrender every wrong done to me.

I will no longer carry the burden of sadness.
He turns my mourning into joy.
The Lord in heaven desires for His children to
be joyous and of a happy heart.

Be of a happy heart and happy in spirit,
for the Lord brings nourishment to the soul.
You are my peace and joy when I'm mourning.
Lift my spirit from the place of sheol
so I may see Your goodness and grace.

Do not hide and cover Your face from me, O Lord.
Do not hide Your presence from Your faithful servant.
Though I am stuck in mind, body, and soul,
the Spirit of the living God within me will never perish.

All else may fail,
but the Word of God is never chained or imprisoned.
Imprisoned you may be,
but the inner man is not bound by the chains and
shackles of hell.
Your spirit shall live for eternity and reign in heaven.

Epic 90

The wonderful and great mysterious God You are.
The giver of life, and the Lord who breathed life into
my mortal body.
You pulled me from man's rib and formed me into the
God-fearing woman you called me to be.

You called me into existence so I can have an intimate
relationship with You.
You are a man, O' God, and the founder of life.
You have blessed me with many things my soul can
hardly bear.

My Lord, You have given me qualities and attributes
tailored to please my husband.
When I look into his eyes, I see the Almighty's spirit
burning ablaze within his soul.
My husband shall be obedient and bind upon his heart
the ordinances and statutes of the Lord.

He shall be a mighty man after God's own heart.
He shall mimic the ways of the Lord.

The Lord shall forever hold my precious and tender heart
in His victorious hand of righteousness.
The Lord's righteousness shall cover me even unto the grave.
Satan knows there is a righteousness
about those who are called.

Satan knows who is after the Lord's heart.
The unjust judge will try to tempt with things of the flesh
and deceitfulness of the eyes
to pull those away from the Father.
The Father knows all secrets.

He knows what is in darkness and shall expose
the evildoers of the night for who they really are.
The brightness of the Lord's Spirit shall
eradicate the darkness of the underworld.

Fill this dark world with Your supreme power and glory.
Cover the earth with Your illuminated Spirit.
Illuminate the most nebulous parts with Your presence.

Demonstrate to mankind that You are sovereign,
and that You have dominion over the universe.
You, O God, are the backbone and founder of creation.
You create everything with a purpose.
In due season, the meaning shall be unveiled.

The Father does not create something without a purpose.
There is a cause and effect for every being God has created.
Therefore, you are not a mistake, my child.

You are a child of the Most High God.
We are the sons and daughters God created in His image.
We were created after God's own precious and sacred heart.

Abba Father's heart is filled with
immaculate, unconditional love.
The Lord's love is not of this world.
It is not love of the flesh, or eros, but rather agape love.

Epic 91

Blessing, honor, and glory is due Your name, O Lord.
Blessed are you who has picked up your cross,
followed the Lord, and kept His ordinances.
The Lord's ordinances and statutes are precious
and should bind them upon their hearts for eternity.

The kingdom of God is for eternity and all
that is within its realm.
The kingdom of God holds the keys to our
destiny and fate.
Hold onto thy faith, dear child, for these are
perilous times in which we reside.

We reside in a world filled with demonic activity
and unadulterated evil in the streets and in the home.
The evil of the night has crept into the hearts and minds
of people.
Do not be imitators of evil,
but rather imitate the goodness of the Lord.

Continue, my child, in the ways of the Lord,
for in its appointed time and season,
you shall reap the rewards of your faithfulness.
Though others mock your obedience and diligence,
the Lord is watching them as well.

My allegiance is not to mankind but to my Father
in heaven.
My obedience and diligence is honored in heaven
before the Lord God Almighty.
Owe no man anything but love.

Love all, even those who persecute you in secret,
for the Lord shall reward you in the
open for your faithfulness.
Be kind and gentle to those who have gone astray.
Be merciful and loving to all who are in dire need.
Do not turn your back on your brother or sister in Christ,
for you may be entertaining an angel.

Treat people with dignity and honor.
Do not look upon others haughtily,
those who may be less fortunate than you,
for when you do, it grieves the Father.

Do not be quick to turn away someone who
does not look a certain way.
Do not be quick to go overboard for someone
who appears to be royalty,
for we are all royalty in the Father's eyes.

We have been created equally.
Do not forsake those who do not possess monetary wealth,
for they are prosperous in mind, body, soul, and spirit.
They are prosperous in the Word of God.

These true servants of His Majesty have a deep yearning
to satisfy the Father.
They moan and have a cry the Father adheres to.
A cry to restore the godless nations.

Nation against nation,
religion against religion.
in the so-called name of God.

Those who slay servants and worshippers of the Lord
shall be held accountable.
Innocent blood has been shed
You shall be judged and condemned for the wicked sacrifices
you have made before these false gods.

The blood of the martyrs is still fresh.
The martyrs cry for vengeance.
Though these martyrs were slain for believing in Christ,
their spirits shall carry a legacy that
will impact many nations.

You can burn me on the cross,
but you cannot destroy the Spirit of God within me.
The Spirit of truth shall abide in me for all eternity.

Epic 92

We serve a God that man nor science can figure out.
We rationalize the thoughts of the Lord God
through our novice intelligence and understanding.

Reveal Your purpose and plan to my spirit.
My spirit and soul yearns for the truth about life.
The Creator of life is a big mystery.

Though we have a deep and personal relationship
with our Savior,
we will never understand the mind and concepts of
His Majesty.
The Lord's thoughts are pure, angelic, and wholesome.
Our thoughts have been polluted by venomous words
of the world.

I desire to have the mind to solve knotty spiritual dilemmas.
We are entering a time when the natural intelligence of man
will no longer be able to rectify the problems of this world.

Desire to be at one with the Father
so He can reveal the hidden mysteries of His kingdom.
The realm of God is filled with ideas,
concepts, and inventions that mankind can barely withstand.
He reveals those precious gifts and spiritual endowments
to true worshippers.

Spiritual endowments are bestowed upon believers for
edification of the church.
The church is to be God's anointed and chosen vessel.
But instead the church is involved in diabolical acts of Satan.

Those churches God has not ordained or
called into existence shall perish at the hands of Satan.
Though you may worship the Devil in secrecy and solitude,
the Lord shall expose you.

The unjust judge may appear to be your friend,
but when the King of Glory judges you,
Satan will leave you in the abyss of eternal damnation.

Satan receives glory from torturing
and tormenting the righteous.
You evildoers of the night, woe to you who follows Satan,
for the Lord shall cast your spirits into the lake of fire
for eternal punishment.

Chuckle now, O wicked one of the night,
for Satan is the author of perversion.
The wicked may think they have gained victory
and glory on earth,
but the Lord does not allow repeat offenders to be set loose.

The righteous shall have the victory and glory on earth.
The unjust will suffer and perish at the hands of Satan.
The wicked shall not only be forsaken by God
but also by the Devil.

The wicked shall yell for mercy,
but the Lord will grant no clemency to the wicked,
for they have forsaken the ways of Christ and followed Baal.
You have indulged in the wickedness of the night,
and you shall be extinguished by the fiery darts of hell.

Epic 93

May the Spirit of the Lord fill this place.
Spirit of truth, guide Your people into the
reverential fear and knowledge of the Lord.
Invade the earth with truth and wisdom, O God.

There are many so-called truths loose in the world.
Many wandering pastors who God did not ordain
are preaching heresy.
Do not believe and adhere to everything you hear, my child.

Not every spirit that speaks of the Lord is of God.
Every word must be tested and tried.
When the Lord speaks, it is comforting and peaceful
to your spirit and soul.

Test the words and spirit of man,
for man is undoubtedly deceitful and wicked.
Man would rather boast to gain recognition
and glory from others.

Do not boast about your achievements and great success,
for when you do, the Lord shall bring you to your knees.
It is the Lord who has given you the power to get wealth.

We cannot perform to the standards God has set,
for we are mere mortals.
Flesh and blood beings who need strength and valor
from the Lord to do the unexpected.

I am nothing without my Lord and Savior.
A mere entity wandering the streets
for a purpose and plan to life.
Our lives are meaningless until we accept Christ.
Christ is the leader and founder of my faith and destiny.
He holds my fate and final destination in His hands.
He is the author and finisher of my life,
not Satan or the unjust judge.

There are many critics and judges among us.
Do not allow their false judgments and malignant words
to corrupt your spirit.

Adhere and hold firm to the ways and words of the Lord.
Even though these critics possess a form of piety,
they have become blinded and detached from the light.

The Word of God brings forth truth and light.
The adversary's purpose is to destroy the Word
within you.
If he can do that, the illumination of God's Word
will be darkened.

Do not allow the obscure ways of Satan to snatch you
from the truth God has spoken unto your spirit.
There will be many dark, boisterous voices in your ear,
but these unjust spirits cannot confiscate the living God
abiding within you.

The inner man the Creator has blessed with
wisdom, might, and power is more catastrophic than
the wickedness of the night.

Though Satan will attempt to attack from every angle,
put on the whole armor of God to withstand the fiery darts.
When these darts try to penetrate
your spirit and separate you
from God,
stand and fight!

You may feel wounded in spirit and soul.
Heartache and despair have covered your being.
Though I cry tears of distress and pain,
I must have the will to go on.

Wretchedness and gloom have covered my soul
since I was an infant.
Battles have consumed my being the majority of my days.
When shall I see the goodness and favor of the Lord?

I pray that my enemies be put to shame.
Break the jaws and teeth of those who desire
that I be put to shame.
Shame shall not cover me,
but it shall cover the wicked.

Epic 94

The Spirit of the Lord shall hover over the universe,
the stars, and cosmos even after Armageddon.
The day of Armageddon shall leave many saddened
and wounded.
Armageddon shall leave many distraught and in despair.

I pray that you will take the road to heaven.
That you, my child, will surrender your wicked ways
to the almighty God.
Our God is faithful and just to forgive us of our sins.

We were once in the darkness,
enslaved to the torment and tortures of hell.
Satan has blinded the world with his sinister, devious plans.

The Devil has put up a veil so mankind will be hindered
from the truth and nature of God's Word.
The unjust judge has many territories,
commanded by demons.
These demons of the night have bewitched many.

Do not allow these demons of the night to
bewitch you with these so-called
signs, wonders, and miracles.
There are many signs and wonders performed among us,
but these wonders are not of God.
Be careful, my child, for there are many loose scoundrels.

Render justice, O God, to those who have endured injustice.
The injustice of this world is not of
God but of the Wicked One.
The Wicked One has imposed unfair acts and injustice
upon the righteous.

Though it appears that the righteous is outnumbered
and defeated by Satan and his massive army, they are not.
Every battle will not end in victory.
Unfortunately, one must suffer hardships
and disappoints in life.

We try to rationalize the things the almighty God does.
No man or science will ever come to
the conclusion of the things
and decisions the Father makes.

We must live our lives to the fullest without regret.
Do not allow Satan to condemn you with past sins.
Dear child, do not allow the burdens of this world
to cause you to lose faith

O faith, what a wonderful gift God has bestowed
upon believers.
Our faith must be tried so we can be a living testimony
to those in crisis.
The pain, trials, and tribulations one
must endure to follow Christ.

The journey that one accepts with Christ is vexatious,
for when we choose to give our lives to Christ,
the gates of hell release havoc.
These demons and creatures from Satan's army
are sent to torment and torture us.

We must not fear Satan or his army,
for he knows the weaknesses of man and will attack
with a ferocious blow.
For evil, wickedness, and murder of the innocent,
the Lord shall bring judgment upon him.

A judgment so devastating and a wrath no beast or human
can withstand will shake the nations.
Do not anger or tempt the Lord your God,
for when you do, the Lord shall evoke
a spiritual death and torture.

Those who were tortured by Satan and his ghouls
will be cast into a dark hole with no
trace of their wretched souls.
Our spirit man reveals the truth and
nature of whose we really are.
On judgment day, many will be saddened by the atrocities
they have committed.

We cannot undo the past,
for it is not who we really are.
We are children of the Most High God
and have been made righteous through the blood of Jesus.

The blood of Jesus is more dynamic than any sin,
for it cleanses our inner being.

Epic 95

Fill the world with Your glory and essence, O God.
Your ways are pure.
The pureness and sanctification within the Father's heart
leads many to repentance.

Father God, forgive Your servants of their sins and iniquities.
Cover our iniquity, shame, and guilt with the blood of Jesus.
The blood of Jesus is more dynamic than any being or foe
upon the face of the earth.

The earth is filled with massive iniquities, injustices,
and atrocities of Satan.
The earth was once filled with the righteousness of
our Lord and Savior.
But Satan has implemented unjust laws to tarnish the
reputation of Christ.

God is the judge, lawgiver, and king over every being.
The Father decides what rules shall be enacted.
Though the Father allows Satan to implement unjust rules
and demonic kingdoms,
the Father ultimately has the final say.

God does not reveal every purpose or plan that will be
put into effect.
He wants us to believe only in the truth of His Word,
despite our circumstances.
Though the things and circumstances of the outside world
may bewilder you,
do not allow them to lead you astray.

Do not allow the adversary to pull you from His Majesty.
Despite the hardships and heartaches of life,
one must still remain faithful.
The Lord your God shall reward your faithfulness
and allegiance to Him.
We must hold fast to our confession of faith,
for God honors our allegiance and dedication.
We have formed an alliance with the powerful Almighty
who none can object to.

Many will come to you in the form of preachers and
worshippers of the living God.
They will impose beliefs upon many with beguilement.
Do not allow your eyes or ears to be fooled
by the venomous words they speak.

Come out from among those who do not worship
the Lord your God.
These sorcerers and witches of the night dabble
in black magic in secrecy.
These people appear to be God-fearing and wholesome.

But underneath their smile and eloquence of speech
lies a ravenous wolf.
Remove the decorative ornaments and tongues
of these devils.

Cast these devils into the pit of destruction so
no one will suffer from their blows.
A tragedy into the cave of no return.

As the righteous of heaven rejoice over their
victorious slaying of Satan and his demonic kingdom,
the unjust shall succumb to the sword of Satan and God.
The injustices inflicted upon the just shall
boomerang unto the graves of the wicked.

The wicked shall yell for clemency,
but the Lord shall turn His back.
They have denied the Father in heaven, and
He shall remove them from His presence.

Every wicked act that you have committed upon earth
shall be judged in heaven.
One must pay for the devilish acts upon the just.
While the righteous remain at peace,
the evildoers will suffer eternal damnation of their souls.

Epic 96

Hear my cry and prayer, O God of David.
You are the God of David who slew Goliath.
A God of devastating force yet loving and tender
to the brokenhearted.

Broken in mind, body, soul, and spirit you may be,
but we serve a God who heals all distress and hurt.
Hurt brought my child to despair,
but he was never abandoned by the Lord.

Abandoned by people of the world but not
forsaken by the Lord.
Tears of melancholy and aching of spirit
have consumed me.
Remove the burden and lashes that Satan has
bestowed upon Your people.

We have been redeemed by the blood of the Lamb.
The injustices of the wicked shall not prevail over the just,
for the Lord of Hosts is the judge, ruler, and lawgiver.

Mankind does not have the final word;
rather, it is our Father in heaven.
Our Father in heaven dictates what shall be done on earth,
not Satan.
Satan is a mere ant in the Lord's eyes.

No man or beast has ever laid eyes on God.
We know of His presence because He
resides within our inner man.
The inner man knows the voice of the Lord.

God's presence is peaceful and restful.
The presence of the Lord eradicates all nebulousness
while in prayer,
for prayer unlocks the hidden mysteries and schemes
of the Wicked One.

Always pray in good and in tumultuous times.
The Lord honors those who adhere to
Him through the raging waters.
Though the sea of death may be trying to drown your spirit,
hold onto God's majestic hand along with the words of power
He injected into your spirit and soul.

Satan only uses the things we are petrified of to destroy us.
Though the outward man may have fears,
the spirit man fears nothing.
God did not give us a spirit of fear but
of power. (2 Timothy 1:7)
Nothing by any means shall hurt you.

Satan will attack from every angle.
The tricks of Satan were manifested before Adam and Eve.
Though Lucifer's schemes may appear creative, they are not.
Same scheme but packaged more subtly.

The Evil One knows what your hearts desires.
He comes in the form of a God-fearer.
Do not allow your eyes and ears to be deceived
by His false works and venomous words.

Do not be lured by the status and riches of the wicked.
Though we desire an abundant life in
mind, body, soul, and spirit,
the riches of this world are vile,
for Satan has polluted the riches of this realm.

When the Lord blesses His servants,
it is through His grace and loving-kindness.
The Lord withholds no good thing.

When Satan blesses, it comes through
heartache and abomination.
One shall pay for these riches through
curses, pestilence, and wretchedness
of the spirit.

Epic 97

Blessed is who keeps the ordinances and statutes of the Lord.
Blessed are they who walk after the spirit and not the flesh.
The flesh is devious and conniving.
No good thing dwells in it.

Dwell in the house of the Lord.
When you do, you shall find the peace
and tranquility of His Highness.
The Lord's ways are angelic and in right standing.

Lord, breathe Your omnipotent presence unto my path.
As you direct my paths, O God,
I become more engrafted in Your Word and presence.
Being in the presence of the Lord brings satisfaction
and fulfillment to my soul.

Penetrate my spirit and soul with Your everlasting Word.
The Word of God is sacred and pure.
Each word the Lord speaks illuminates the darkness
and obliterates all wickedness of the night.

Do not allow the momentous things of this world
to tarnish your faith.
Do not allow the malevolent creatures of the underworld
to confiscate the precious words God
has spoken into your spirit.

Though we are among evildoers,
do not allow their vile words and ways to sway you
from the truth.
Do not allow Satan to con you into
thinking there is another truth.

Satan has blinded many with sorcery and black magic
to cover and hide the truth.
No entity, being, or beast can hide from
the presence of the Father.
The Father knows what dwells in the darkness,
for He is the Creator of heaven and hell.

Turn from your wicked ways and pursue righteousness.
Do not allow the adversary to tempt you with things
from the dark side.

Cover those, O God, who are lost and
blinded by Satan's words.
Release those who are enslaved to the darkness.
Send forth a catastrophic war to those in Satan's army.

Annihilate those who desire to do evil and persecute
those who shed innocent blood.
Seal shut the mouths of those who spread hate
and bigotry toward Your kingdom.

No kingdom or empire shall surpass the throne of
the Lord.
The Father's throne is set on high for eternity.
The subjects on the land can overthrow a king,
but no person, duke or commoner,
can overthrow His Majesty
because He is the King of Kings.

It is written, "As I live, said the Lord, every knee shall bow
to me and every tongue shall confess to God." (Romans 14:11)
Though you have to be faithful and loyal to an earthly king,
your allegiance is to the Father in heaven.
He is the one and only true King that reigns over all.

Every great empire was appointed for
a specific time in history.
These empires conquered much.
Though these kings had a marvelous reign on earth,
their reign eventually came to an end.

While kings slaughter one another to
mark history and territory,
the King of Kings is the Creator and founder of history.
While some kings go unremembered for centuries,
we serve a King who was reigning before He said,
"Let there be light!" (Genesis 1:3)

Epic 98

Guide those, O God, who are lost in the wilderness of despair.
Despair and hopelessness have consumed the earth
the Lord God has created.
I desire to be at one within myself.

I desire to be whole and healthy because
it is my covenant right.
Christ's death was not in vain.
He was crucified so we may have an
intimate and personal relationship with Him.

Health, wholeness, and abundance is what the
body of Christ desires.
He was bruised, beaten, and crucified to save us
from eternal damnation.
The lashes and markings forced upon our Lord
were so we could be free from sin and the death penalty.

The death penalty is a form of eternal
punishment one should not want to adhere to.
Adhere to the ways of the Lord,
for in doing so, you shall reap a harvest.
A harvest of eternal life and peace from the adversary.

Satan's objective is to ruin one's peace and disrupt
the Holy Spirit from performing miracles in one's life.
Our life is not dictated by the things of the flesh
but by the Word spoken by the Holy Spirit.

Holy Spirit, rest upon those who delight
in keeping Your statutes.
Speak life and power into those who have wandered
onto the path of destruction.
Send forth divine protection, and witness to those, my Lord,
who are enslaved in the camp of despair.

Stir up the gifts and the blood of the righteous.
Call forth those, my Lord, who are under the curse
of the Wicked One.
No curse is too robust compared to the wrath
that is encased in Abba Father's Spirit.

The Spirit of the Lord is so dynamic that it
shakes the spirits of the dead.
Though the dead are silent in their graves,
they still cry out and praise Abba Father.
We serve a God whose Spirit carries a legacy and honor
no demon can withstand.

False gods and carved wooden idols lack life and power
to transform storms into peaceful journeys.
These false gods are spiritless and shall be cast
unto the dogs of the night.

The dogs of the night shall feed upon the flesh of those
who delight in devilry.
The spirits and souls of the wicked shall suffer
eternal damnation and persecution.
Suffering for the Lord is one thing,
but the wicked shall suffer by the hand of God.

The hand of God holds the keys to eternal life
and punishment.
The hand of the almighty God is so grand
that He controls the earth's axis.
Time and dominion are controlled by the
Almighty's presence.

In the Father's presence is richness and sanctity.
The more you desire to be in His presence,
the more He will reveal His precious secrets.
Hidden secrets and treasures are preserved
for those who desire to please the Lord with righteousness.

Righteousness shall clothe you even unto judgment day.
Judgment day will be filled much sorrow for the wicked.
But those in right standing with God shall rejoice
and be at rest from all persecution.

Persecution shall not cover the righteous on judgment day.
But the persecution and fiery darts
shall puncture and wound
the spirits of the ungodly.
You shall suffer spiritual wounds for eternity.
Wounds that will never heal but rather
deepen from hell's fire.

Epic 99

The Lord encamps around those who fear Him.
Fear the Lord with all Your heart, mind, soul, and spirit.
The Spirit of the Lord is with those who are broken
and of a wounded soul.

Consume the wicked with a fire that shall set
their spirits ablaze.
Consume them, O Lord, with a wrath that shall
be felt in their graves.
The Lord shall cause calamity to come upon evildoers.
The Lord is a Spirit-filled being that knows all.
God's Spirit is so robust that the dead will be
awakened by His presence on judgment day.

Armageddon is a day that shall shake the nations.
A day of melancholy for the wicked,
but a day of rejoicing for the righteous,
for Satan shall be put to eternal shame and damnation.

Darkness encamps around those who dabble in the occult.
The occult is filled with lies, deceit, and diabolical acts.
But the Lord's presence is light in dark places.

The light of the Lord surrounds those who reverently
worship and fear Him.
Respect and honor the Father in heaven,
for in Him is the richness and fulfillment of life.

Breathe Your omniscient power and Spirit, my Lord,
into my presence.
Purge my heart of all wickedness, and fill my soul
with unconditional love.
Shower my spirit and soul, O God, with everlasting
peace and sanctification.

Sanctify and consecrate my spirit and soul away
from the world.
Do not allow the things of this demonic world
to pull you asunder and uproot the truth you have learned.
The truth is in the words God has revealed unto your spirit

The truth is in the Bible,
for it is prophetically spoken and written by His Majesty.
The truth lies in Abba Father's mouth.
Every word the Lord speaks is powerful and Spirit-filled.

The Lord created the tongue for a purpose.
Rather than utilizing one's tongue to destroy yourself,
use your tongue to devour the kingdom of darkness.

Satan's objective is for the body of Christ to quarrel
with one another.
If he can get you to speak against your brother,
he has your tongue.
Do not allow Satan to exploit your words.

Our mouths are weapons that can cause
catastrophic storms.
Refrain your tongue against your neighbor.
Allow the Holy Spirit to make utterances through you.

The Holy Spirit has spoken utterances unto your
spirit that cannot be taken from you.
Praise our Father in heaven,
for He has given us the spirit of Him.
In God lies the truth about Christ.

Christ is the Father above all nations.
Every nation shall bow and confess that our
Lord reigns over all.
He reigns over the moon, the stars, the cosmos,
and every other element.

In God lies the creation of earth and mankind.
Humanity would not be in existence had the
Lord not created us in His image.
He has handpicked us saints of God.

You reign on high, my Lord.
Your rod and staff has punctured the evildoers
in their souls.
You punish the wicked with calamity.
But with the righteous, You show Yourself mighty.

You punish the wicked with the rod of chastisement.
But with the godly, Your rod and staff are
protection and redemption from the curse of the law.

Epic 100

When I praise You, Master in heaven, it brings
joy and peace to my soul.
Your presence, O Lord, keeps me rooted and
grounded in Your Word.
Your words, O God, bring laughter unto my soul.

Laughter and the oil of joy are the blessed endowments
of the Father to His children.
You gird Your children, my Lord, with the
breastplate of righteousness.
You have taken me by the hand, Father, and
guided me into unconditional love.

A love that no human can put asunder,
the Lord's love is very gentle and tender.
The love of our Father shines light in our darkness.

The light of the Lord is a beacon to those who
are lost in the wilderness.
Though I may veer off the path of righteousness,
my eyes and ears know the voice of the Lord.

His Majesty has a Spirit that awakens the sleeping giant.
Though we grow weary in the natural,
our spirits are filled with the knowledge and strength
of our Father.
Guard my strength and might,
for I shall have need of it.

Thunder and hailstones surround the Majesty's throne.
The Lord's temple is filled with wisdom,
knowledge, and miracles stored for the righteous.
The words and ways of the righteous are light to
those who are enslaved in Satan's camp.

As you soar from the heavens, my Lord,
You bring justice to the righteous.
The righteous are afflicted for bearing and carrying
the name of Christ.
Though the heathen nations renounce God,
the faithful and just shall inherit eternal life.

Fidelity, honor, and the admiration we show the
Father reflects our relationship with Him.
The Lord is with those who worship Him in spirit and truth.
Honor our Father in heaven,
for He is the Creator of every good and angelic being.

The angels of the Lord encamp around those who fear Him.
Fear the Lord with all your heart, mind, and soul.
Honoring the ways and statutes of the Lord
shows we are children of the Most High God.

We serve a God who is divine.
No weapon formed against His Majesty shall penetrate the
kingdom of the almighty God.
The almighty God reigns on high and soars in the heavens.
His Spirit is felt in the uttermost parts of the earth.

When God is rejected in nations,
He manifests Himself in ways that are unexplainable.
He shows Himself mighty in the eyes of the unbelieving.
There is no other god like Him.
The stars and cosmos bow at His command.

The universe bows at the Father's feet,
for He is the Alpha and Omega over every being.
In God lies the creation of truth.
Without the Spirit of truth,
the world would be beguiled by Satan's perversion.

With the wicked, Lord, You show Yourself
merciless and tyrannical.
But with the just, You show Yourself gentle and loving.
Those who have offended the Lord shall succumb to the
torture of the underworld.

Just as you have ruled the poor with need
and the just with your so-called rod of chastisement,
the Lord shall evoke a sentence upon you that is irrevocable,
a sentence that the unjust judge cannot abolish.
The Lord is King of Kings and Lord of Lords.
He is the judge who determines our fate.

Run, O Wicked One, from the judge in heaven,
for you shall have to give an account of every wicked deed.
Your wickedness shall follow you even unto your grave.
Your evil shall consume your soul and spirit for eternity.

You shall cry unto the Lord for clemency and salvation
on judgment day,
but the Lord shall turn a deaf ear.
The Lord hears the cries and moans of the just,
but He seals the cries of the wicked with eternal damnation.

Epic 101

You open heaven's gates with Your omnipotent presence
along with a splendid Spirit that lives for eternity.
The heavens and the angels of God's armies
bow at the sound of Abba Father's voice.
The voice of the Lord humbles the arrogant.

The arrogant shall be brought unto their knees
for their haughty looks upon the poor.
Poor in the natural you may be but rich and
fruitful in the Word and Spirit of the Lord.
The Lord encamps around those who
are oppressed by the Wicked One.

Injustices have been evoked upon the righteous
by demons of the night.
These demons rule the oppressed with unjust
laws along with a demonic government.
These wicked rulers hold high status in society.

The wicked believe they are exempt from the rules of heaven.
Though you may be a ruler or judge on earth,
the Lord is the supreme judge and ruler over every entity.
Though you attempt to enslave the just and the
poor to satanic rule,
you, O Wicked One, shall give an account to the Lord
for every vile act.

Unleash Your rage and wrath, O God, on the oppressor.
Release plagues, earthquakes, and
hurricanes upon the demoniacs.
These demoniacs possess authority that has bewitched
the eyes of many.

Sorcery, beguilement, and enchantments have
vexed those who lack the truth in their nature of God's Word.
Do not be misled, my child, by false prophecies
and so-called miracles manifested by demons.
Demons possess powers,
for they are servants to the Prince of Darkness.
But the powers that are found in the Father's belly
will subdue the powers of Baal.

Though Satan possesses the authority to transform
one's life for the better,
you shall have to render your soul and
spirit unto him for fame.
When ye cross unto the dark side, the Lord shall be the judge,
for He is the Creator of heaven and hell.

Hell is filled with wretchedness and despair
along with the torture and torment of ghouls.
There is no escaping the fiery darts of hell in the afterlife.
The afterlife of the wicked shall be consumed
with the pestilence of Satan.

Pestilence, murder, and deceit are of the accuser.
The Antichrist is a deceiver of many.
He sends forth many deluded miracles
along with devilish prophecies.

Do not be vexed by the eloquence of speech
and religious talk in these last days.
Many will be deceived by the signs, wonders,
and miracles of the adversary.
The adversary has unleashed a war upon the
kingdom of God.

Both kingdoms are battling for supremacy and
sole control of your spirit and soul.
Which kingdom shall you serve?
Serve the kingdom of heaven.
Then you shall have a peaceful journey into paradise on
judgment day.

I shall praise the Lord in the fiery furnace of affliction.
Though I may be rejected for bearing
the name of Jesus Christ,
my fidelity I owe unto my Father.

Curses and blessings have proven me to a true servant
of the Lord.
A servant of the Lord I am.
I am bound in servitude unto His Majesty for eternity.

I pray that You, O Lord, manifest the glory
that abides in me to many nations.
The nations shall feel the presence of the Lord.

I shall speak with such profound and godly wisdom
that it will remove the barriers of hatred.
Though I carry a heavy mantle,
the Spirit of the Lord causes me to remain still in the
fiery furnace with no blazing of spirit.

Conclusion

We often question God's existence and His unconditional love for us. We are put in tumultuous situations to test our strength and faith in the Almighty. These trying situations at times push us away from the Father.

After I took ill for a few years, my spirit and soul grew weary from the lashes and whips of life. Our lives our predestined, whether for good or ill. Through illness, I found the inner strength to propel myself toward my God-given destiny. Through tears of distress, melancholy, and anger, I found the will to go on.

The bruises and marks from adversity that the child of the Most High God must endure mold us into God-fearing warriors. Hurt and brought to despair you may be, but adhere to the words spoken unto thy spirit. Satan can confiscate all items from your life, but he cannot remove the engrafted Word of God that was injected into your soul. Thanks be to our Lord Jesus Christ! I pray that through my pain, grief, and sorrow these writings puncture the hearts and souls of mankind.